DINERS' DICTIONARY

DAWN AND DOUGLAS NELSON

ITALIAN

DINERS' DICTIONARY
DAWN AND DOUGLAS NELSON

ITALIAN

PROTEUS
London & New York

PROTEUS BOOKS is an imprint of
The Proteus Publishing Group

United Kingdom
PROTEUS (PUBLISHING) LIMITED
Bremar House,
Sale Place,
London, W2 IPT.

United States
PROTEUS PUBLISHING CO., INC.

distributed by
CHARLES SCRIBNER'S SONS
597 Fifth Avenue
New York, N.Y. 10017

ISBN O 906071 33 X

First published in U.K. Sept. 1980
First published in U.S. Sept. 1980
© 1980 by Dawn and Douglas Nelson and
Proteus Publishing Company
All rights reserved.

Printed and bound in Great Britain
at The Pitman Press, Bath

INTRODUCTION

This Is *Not* A Cookery Book Or A List Of Recipes

It is a *Dictionary* to be carried and used when confronted with a menu in an Italian eating establishment of any grade anywhere in the World. It is strictly Alphabetical.

Look up the first word of the menu dish; if it does not give the full answer, look up the second *main* word and so on.

The short specialty section is for the traveller in Italy.

The wine section is for guidance only and not an authoritative discourse and could be of value to the traveller or to the purchaser of Italian wine elsewhere.

This has been produced as an aid to ourselves. From menus over a number of years we have collected French, Italian and other national gastronomic terms by means of scribbling surreptitiously into a notebook, whilst carefully avoiding the glare of suspicious waiters. It is bad enough not knowing how a dish is to be prepared but it is a disaster to receive something totally unexpected. Once in France after confidently ordering a light soup we were eventually greeted with a highly-spiced sausage dish as a precurser to a large rich main dish; the light dry wine did not exactly compliment the sausage. This book sets out to avoid such calamities. There are, of course, many excellent books produced for the professional but most of these start with the basic premise that you know quite a lot about cooking (which we do — but never enough) and that you are aware at what part of the menu the named dish occurs — almost all these books divide into Soups, Hors d'oeuvres, Fish etc. In Italy, in particular, the menu may well be written in longhand with additional dishes pushed in, not necessarily in the right order, as they become available; this raises some doubt as to where to find it and by the time one has searched through a number of sections it is quicker to order and find out.

The classic difficulty can, however, arise with something like Lumache, which is a form of pasta shaped like snail shells but which can also mean the real thing — both appear early in the meal and could be regarded as "starters" or could appear in different sections if pastas are separated. We happen to like either but it is nice to appreciate beforehand that the word can mean both! This book is, therefore simply in straightforward alphabetical order because time after time the same word can occur with different meanings on the same menu.

The Italians are great individualists which is one of the reasons that we frequently have similar interprative problems to theirs; a word can mean any number of things according to the area you happen to be in. For example, Coppa which the dictionary informs us means cup or goblet: In Parma it refers to shoulder of pork, in Rome to brawn and, in Veneto to a form of meat loaf. Later on in the menu it emerges as the French Coupe, being a mixture of ices and fruit. In the same way there will be no slavish adherence to a specified form of cooking nor rigid use of only the identified items in a named dish. If the cook feels like changing a few things he will, though the dish will retain its standard name; if it is the way Mamma made it then that is good enough and he will acknowledge no other authority. One is inclined to imagine that the French are much more rigid and that a specified name will be universal at international restaurants throughout the world. Only too often if one refers to standard text books this is not the case; for instance a garnish may have more than one definition as in the "à la Catalane".

Compared to French, however, Italian has many more variables particularly as the first word may refer to the cut of meat and the rest of the description can be applied to five or more different parts of the joint. Thus, although the Italian Dictionary is a companion to the French Diners' Dictionary, it must differ from it in many respects. A great number of dishes are common to both cuisines but even the most biased Italian would admit that the international nomenclature is largely French and the Italians have frequently adopted the French name and given it their own spelling & pronounciation. The names for classic French dishes are usually short and thus easily referred to in the appropriate work particularly as many English-speaking people are familiar with many of the words.

The Italian menu can however, be more of a problem in that the dish may be described by a number of words — none of which is familiar. Thus the appearance of MANZO LESSO IN POLPETTE ALLA ROMANA under the French system would require reference to each word which would be laborious — so in this book each word is individually defined but some of the better known dishes such as this are recorded in full under the first letter of the first word — in this case under MANZO. When the main content appears as a latter word some difficulty may arise thus INTINGOLO DI MAIALE E UCCELLETTI ALLA TOSCANA does in fact occur under INTINGOLO which means "cut in pieces" rather than MAIALE meaning "pork" to prevent the MAIALE section becoming overloaded and thus difficult to locate dishes. It will also occur under Toscana. Sometimes, when a dish such as NOCCIOLE D'AGNELLO ALL'ITALIANA appears on the menu as COSTOLETTINE D'AGNELLO ALL'ITALIANA, the system of referring to individual words is the only way of identifying its constituents and method of preparation. A small pocket reference such as this cannot, of course, be fully comprehensive and the duplication of entries puts some strain on available space. Occasions may arise when the French book will be needed but to cover this eventuality would have made both volumes too large to satisfy the essential requirement of making a visit to Italy or an Italian 'ristorante' more enjoyable and any surprises, pleasant one.

There is a small Regional Specialty Section of Italy at the end of the book but we have not found this to be as important in Italy as in France and for the latter have felt it necessary to devote a complete volume to the regions. There are vast differences in climate, people, language and food in the areas of Italy but with each passing year these probably get less and the fine autostrada system has done much towards this; when one tries to analyze the differences it is possible to find major alterations from village rather than region to region and the only advice is to enjoy the surprises you meet. Even the old belief that rice and risottos were mainly of the north and pastas of the south can no longer be regarded as a rule.

This book should be of use in Italian restaurants all over the world as there will be some basic resemblances in the Italian menus wherever produced although in one's own country the interpretation should be available — but to the traveller the Italian restaurant in Greece can offer a problem and this dictionary will be useful. Be warned not always to believe that the 'trattoria' will be quite like that of one's home country — it may be better, it may be worse — it will certainly be different. We recently dined at a much publicized 'ristorante' in a famous tourist center City in southern England. The smoked salmon advertised on its current menu was 'off', the waiter would not bring a particular white wine, Est! Est! Est! as he assured us the ladies would not like it, and at the end of the meal had no cheese board because 'cheese comes in on Tuesdays'. You will seldom find such things in Italy — they would be out of business in no time.

As we have emphasized in the French Introduction, this is *NOT*:

      a)   A cookery book.
      b)   A list of recipes.

it is a guide to the type of materials and method of cooking that a particular name on a menu should turn out to be. Deficiencies must be apparent as nobody could possibly describe CIMA or OSSO BUCO in a few English words — we have done our best.

Dawn and Douglas Nelson
January, 1980

ACKNOWLEDGEMENTS

To every kitchen, cook, chef, waiter and waitress that has fed us well and not minded being asked silly questions. We have seldom been rebuffed and have always had a laugh even when language problems have made the answer incomprehensible — it is inconceivable that in Italian islands we have eaten donkey as often as we inferred from the graphic, vociferous almost hysterical descriptions. To all who prepare and serve food for our delight we say "Thank You".

A large number of books have been consulted over the years in an effort to check accuracy, which must be acknowledged as they are constant resolvers of difficulties.

ELIZABETH DAVID's Italian Food of which our current copy is dated 1966 and cost 5/- — that was great value for money. Even if you are not interested in food it is marvellous reading and to the compulsive eater, a treasure house.

Great Italian Cooking by LUIGI CARNACINA is a much thumbed book both from its service in our kitchen and as a reference: it explains the occurrence for definition of a number of dishes called after Luigi Veronelli, the author's friend and "Villa Sassi" the author's house. When seen on a menu they are recommended.

ENRICA AND VERNON JARRATT's Complete Book of Pasta has a constant place on our bookshelf as does TOM STOBART's Herbs, Spices and Flavourings.

We only recently discovered SPIKE AND CHARMIAN HUGHES' Eating Italian and it is clear they faced the same problems as ourselves. We wish we had found it earlier.

Many books have been consulted on the complicated scenario of Italian wines but the final authority encompassing its expertise into such a compressed field has been The World Atlas of Wine by HUGH JOHNSON, and finally to GUY WHITAKER whose expertise on wine matches his other considerable abilities, we offer thanks for reading and amending the wine sections.

A

ABBACCHIO	Baby lamb.
al Forno:	Roasted with rosemary & garlic.
ABRUZZESE	In the style of Abruzzi.
Cosciotto d'agnello all':	Leg of lamb braised with rosemary, garlic, white wine & tomatoes.
ACCADEMICA Ananasso all':	Cold pineapple with oranges, strawberries, Aurum liqueur & whipped cream.
ACCIUGHE	Anchovies. Small sea fish. Available in Italy whole & salted as well as canned in oil.
alla Carabiniera:	Literally "policeman". A cold antipasta. Anchovies, potatoes, onions, olives in a salad.
alla contadina:	Literally "countryman or peasant". A cold antipasta. Anchovies, parsley, capers, onions & olives stuffed with anchovy butter.
fresche:	Marinaded fresh anchovies.
marinate:	Marinaded fresh anchovies.
in Teglia:	Anchovies baked in oil, garlic & breadcrumbs.
fritte al limone:	Fried. With lemon.
ACETO	Vinegar.
ACETOSA	Sorrel. Similar to spinach. Rumex acetosa or other species.
AFFETTATI MISTI	Mixed cold meats.
AFFOGATO	Poached
AFFUMICATE	Smoked. e.g. herrings.

DINERS' DICTIONARY

AGLIATA	Garlic sauce. Garlic, breadcrumbs, oil & vinegar.
AGLIO	Garlic.
AGNELLO	Lamb. In Italy, sheep under one year old.
Bracioline d':	Sliced & fried.
Brodettato:	Small cubes stewed in wine with egg yolks & cheese.
Cosciotto d':	Leg.
Costoletto-ini d':	Rib chops of lamb or mutton.
Nocciole d':	Small steaks. French "noisette".
Quadrello d':	Loin and best-end.
Quarto d':	Leg.
alla Romana:	Cubed & baked in spiced crumbs.
Spalla d':	Shoulder.
con pisello alla Toscana:	Pot-roasted leg with garlic & rosemary inserted in skin. Tomatoes & oil. Peas.
AGNOLOTTI	A rounded pasta parcel of white meat & cheese filling. Meat & vegetable sauce (Sugo di carne all'Italiana). The same as Ravioli but ravioli must contain the soft sheep's cheese, ricotta. Agnolotti need not.
AGONI	Lake sardines. Small freshwater fish of Lake Como — Alosa lacustris. As antipasta. Cooked in oil & marinaded in vinegar & wild thyme.
AGRODOLCE	Sweet-sour sauce. Wine, pine nuts, sultanas, sugar, vinegar — maybe chocolate — sometimes candied peel, cherries & redcurrant jelly.
Lipre in:	Hare with sweet-sour sauce.
AGUGLIE	Garfish or needle fish. A long thin sea fish with green bones.
ALBICOCCHE	Apricots.
conde:	Hot sweet with creamed rice.

ITALIAN

con crema Inglesa:	Cold. With custard, raspberries, strawberries & maraschino.
deliziose "Lily":	Cold. With almonds, orange juice & chocolate.
Ninon:	Cold. With almonds, blackcurrant jelly, kirsch & cream.
alla Reale:	Cold. With kirsch, aniseed liqueur, raspberries, sponge cake & nuts.
al kümmel:	Iced cold purée with kümmel, macaroons, ice cream, cream & almonds.
ALETTE	Wing of bird.
di Tacchino Dorate:	Fried turkey wings. In breadcrumbs.
di Tacchino Dorate alla Nizzarda:	As above with tomatoes, garlic, black olives & mushrooms.
ALICI	Alternative name of anchovies (ACCIUGHE).
ALKERMES	Italian liqueur of brandy, mace, nutmeg, cloves & cinnamon. Bright red in color.
ALLODOLE	Larks.
ALLORO	Bay leaves.
ALOSA	Shad. A sea water fish of the herring family.
ALZAVOLA	Teal. A small wild duck.
AMARETTI	Macaroons.
AMATRICIANA Spaghetti all':	Spaghetti with bacon & tomatoes. Often corrupted to (ALLA MATRICIANA)!
AMERICANA	French "Américaine".
Astaco all':	Lobster pieces fried in butter with brandy, pepper & white wine. Fish & lobster sauce.
Bistecche all':	Raw minced fillet of beef with egg yolk, onion, sauce, brandy & capers.

DINERS' DICTIONARY

Delizie all':	A savory. Toast with flour, milk, yolk & lemon (Bastard) sauce with anchovy paste & capers.
Fagiano all':	Pheasant grilled spatchcock in breadcrumbs with mushrooms, tomatoes & parsley butter.
ANANASSO	Pineapple.
all'Accademica:	Cold. With oranges, strawberries, Aurum liqueur & whipped cream.
Caralmellato con liquori:	Hot. Prepared at table. Orange juice, brandy, kirsch, Aurum liqueur, sugar & butter to glaze. Possibly ice cream.
all'Italiana:	Cold. Kirsch, strawberries.
in Sorpresa:	Meaning "surprise". Cold. Rum & rum ice cream.
"Villa Sassi":	Hot. Prepared at table. Sliced pineapple with rum, Aurum liqueur, kirsch, hot chocolate sauce, almonds & ice cream.
ANATROC-COLO	Duckling.
ANELLINI	Tiny pasta rings as soup garnish.
ANELLITTI	Ring of cuttlefish, oven cooked. (Sicily).
ANETO	Dill. A herb.
ANGIOLA TERESA	Angela Theresa.
Cappone in casseruola:	Capon stuffed with parsley. Cream, foie gras, egg, ham & white wine.
ANGUILLA	Eels.
alla Azzali:	Pieces fried. With tomatoes, garlic & breadcrumbs.
fresca alla Borgognona:	Hot or Cold. Pieces in oil, garlic & shallots. Brandy, anchovy butter. As an antipasta.

ITALIAN

fresca alla Fiamminga:	Hot or Cold. Pieces fried with sorrel, watercress & herbs. Egg yolk, cream & white wine. As an antipasta.
fresca con cipolline e funghi:	Hot or Cold. Pieces in oil, garlic & white onions. With mushrooms.
alla moda del fattore:	Fried in breadcrumbs. With mustard sauce.
in guazzetta con peperoni e cipolline:	Mixed with yellow peppers & white onions.
alla Provenzale:	Fried with parsley, onion & garlic. Breadcrumbs.
alla Tartara:	Hot. With tartare sauce.
al vino rosso:	Hot. In red wine. With fried bread.
ANICE	The herb Pimpinella anisum from which aniseed is obtained.
Biscotti all':	Aniseed biscuits or cookies.
ANIMELLA DI VITELLO	Veal sweetbreads. Pancreas of calf.
bonne maman:	Casseroled with celery, carrots & onions. White wine.
con carciofi:	Fried with artichokes.
alla diavola:	With tomatoes. Wine & pepper sauce.
fritta al limone:	Fried. Lemon juice & lemons.
die gourmets:	With truffles. As a pie.
alla maître d'hôtel:	Braised with tomatoes & parsley butter.
al proscuitto con purea di patate con salsa piccante:	With ham & mashed potatoes & piquant sauce.

DINERS' DICTIONARY

ANITRA	Duck.
all'Arancia:	Roast with orange sauce.
Arrostita:	Roast.
Brasata con leuticchie:	Braised with lentils.
Brasata con olive verdi:	Braised with green olives.
Brasata con piselli e lardoneini:	Braised with peas & diced pork.
Brasata con rape:	Braised with turnips.
Brasata farcita ed arrostita:	Roast, stuffed with liver, apple & herbs.
ANTICA	French "á l'ancienne". Literally "old lady".
Blanquette di vitello all'antica:	Veal stew with herbs, vegetables & cream.
ANTIPASTO	Literally before the meal. French "hors d'oeuvres", English "starters". Can be hot or cold.
alla Casalinga:	Peppers, tomatoes, onions, dressing, fish in oil. Cold.
Fantasia:	Oysters, shrimps, cream, mayonnaise, sherry, lemon. With celery.
alla Genovese:	Raw board or shell beans, salami & cheese.
di Ortaggi:	Truffles, mushrooms, artichokes, fennel, peppers, celery, pickles, dressing.
Quaresimale:	Cold carp. Eggs, mushrooms, artichokes, olives & mayonnaise.
AQUATOCCA	Vegetable broth. Egg soaked bread. (Tuscany).
ARAGOSTA	Lobster of the Mediterranean or Crawfish. French "Langouste". "Spiny Lobster". Similar to American "Rock lobster." Many recipes — most with

	French derivations. See under ASTACO.
ARANCIA — E alla Madrilena:	Oranges. Orange pudding made with rice.
ARETINA Cosciotto d'agnello all':	Roast leg of lamb. With garlic, red wine & rosemary marinade.
ARIGUSTA	Alternative name of Mediterranean lobster — see ARAGOSTA above.
ARUBGGE	Herrings.
affumicate in insalata:	Smoked herring salad.
salate del Ghiottone:	Salt herring fillets with onions, shallots, parsley, basil, celery & mayonnaise.
salate marinate:	Marinaded salt herring.
salate alla Semplice:	Salt herrings alone.
salate alla Scandinava:	In vinegar with herbs. Rollmops.
ARISTA	Roast (loin of pork).
di Maiale con cardi:	With cardoons.
di Maiale alla Toscana:	With black-eyed beans.
Fiorentina:	Roasted in water with garlic & rosemary & cloves.
Perugina:	As above but fennel instead of rosemary.
ARRABBIATA Penne all':	Pasta with tomatoes, bacon, onion, garlic & chillies.
ARROSTA-INIO	Roasted.
Annegati al vino Bianco:	Roast veal chops in white wine.
Branzino:	Roast bass with white wine (Bercy) sauce.

DINERS' DICTIONARY

Cosciotto d'agnello:	Roast leg of lamb.
ARSELLE	Local Genoa name for small clams (VONGOLE).
ARZAVIKA	Teal. A small wild duck.
ASIAGO	Skimmed cows cheese. From the Veneto.
ASOARAGU	Asparagus.
all'Agro di limone:	With lemon sauce.
di campoal burro e alici:	With anchovy butter.
alla Fiamminga:	French "Flamande". With butter & hot boiled eggs.
all'Italiana:	With cheese & nut butter.
con maionese e panna montata:	With mayonnaise.
alla Maltese:	With a white orange sauce.
alla Milanese:	Cheese, nut butter & fried eggs.
alla Polonese:	With boiled eggs & parsley.
alla Zabaione:	With sauce of egg yolk, white wine & butter.
ASTACO	Lobster or river crayfish.
all'Americano:	French "Américaine". Pieces fried in butter with brandy, pepper & white wine. Fish sauce.
alla Bordolese:	Fried in butter & brandy. Tomato sauce.
al Brandy:	Grilled & flamed in brandy.
alla Crema:	Pieces fried in butter & brandy., With cream & pilaff rice.
alla Diavola:	Oven cooked with mustard sauce.
Fredda in "Bella Vista":	Cold in aspic with lettuce, truffles, vegetables, tarragon & mayonnaise.
Fredda alla Russa:	Cold in aspic with truffles, caviar & Russian salad.
Freddo all'Italian:	Cold with eggs, lettuce, capers, tomatoes & basil. Mayonnaise.

ITALIAN

alla Luigi Veronelli:	Grilled with creamy herb (Béarnaise) sauce.
Maria Jose di Savoia:	Grilled with egg & vegetable sauce. Brandy.
alla Newbourg:	Cut pieces fried. Madeira, eggs, cream & paprika.
Piccante Umberto di Savoia:	Grilled with herbs & mustard.
alla Thermidor:	Oven cooked. With mustard & a cheese sauce.
Villa Sassi:	Grilled with vermouth, marsala, cream, onion & pepper sauce.
ASTICCIOLE	On a spit.
di pollo "Villa Sassi":	Pieces of chicken, ham & sage on skewers. White wine, tomatoes & truffles. Served with pasta (Tagliarini).
AURUM	Orange flavored liqueur.
AZZALI Anguilla alla:	Pieces of eel fried. With tomatoes, garlic & breadcrumbs.

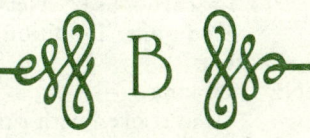

B

BABA AL RHUM	A cake of yeast-leavened dough, raisins & rum.
BACCA	Berry.
BACCALA	Dried Cod.
alla Barcarola:	Stewed in oil with onions, parsley & white wine.
alla Bolognese:	Strips sauteed with onions, garlic, parsley & pepper.

DINERS' DICTIONARY

alla Cappuccina:	Flaked & baked with cheese & potatoes.
fritto Dorato:	Pieces fried in batter in deep oil. Lemon & parsley.
Fiorentina:	Fried in oil with garlic. Tomato sauce.
in Guazzetto alla Romana:	Cooked in oil & garlic. With tomatoes, raisins & pine nuts.
Mantecato:	Creamy mass after pounding with oil. Similar to French "brandade". Specialty of Venice.
alla Napoletana:	Strips cooked in oil. Garlic, tomatoes, black olives, capers & oregano.
con olive verdi:	With tomatoes, gherkins, green olives & capers.
con peperoni alla Romana:	Strips in oil with tomatoes, yellow peppers & onions.
alla Pizzaiola:	Baked with tomatoes & mixed herbs on top.
al Raggio di Sole:	Oven baked with onions, garlic, capers, pine nuts, raisins & anchovy paste.
BAGIOI	Snails with mint & tomato sauce.
BAGNA CAUDA	A hot dip of garlic, anchovies & truffles for cardoons or celery. Specialty of Piedmont. Traditional on Christmas Eve.
BANANE	Bananas.
desiderio di Eva:	Oven cooked with rum, maraschino, Aurum liqueur & cream. With almond macaroons.
infiammati all'Armagnac:	Prepared at table. With orange, maraschino & cream. Flamed in brandy.
infiammati al kirsch:	Flamed in kirsch. Can be cold.
Lucullo:	Skin filled with baked banana mashed

ITALIAN

	with eggs, apricot sauce & curacao.
sciroppato al brandy:	Orange & lemon & brandy flamed.
BARBA-BIETOLA	Beetroot or beet.
aromatizzate con aceto:	Baked & cold in herb vinegar. Antipasta.
alla Besciamella:	Baked & sliced. With white (Béchamel) sauce.
alla crema:	Baked & sliced. With cream.
con erbe fini:	With fresh chopped herbs.
all'Inglese:	Boiled.
marinate alla Russa:	Sliced & alternated with grated horseradish in vinegar. Cold antipasta.
alla Parmigiana:	With meat sauce & parmesan cheese.
BARCAROLA Baccala alla:	Dried cod stewed in oil with onions, parsley & white wine.
BARCHETTE	Tartlets.
di animella di agnello: di animella di vitello:	Lamb or veal sweetbread tartlets with white sauce & sherry.
con Ciliege:	Sour cherry & almond tartlets.
di funghi mornay:	Mushroom tartlets with cheese sauce.
di gamberetti:	Shrimp tartlets with white sauce.
alla Romana:	Chicken, truffles & mushroom tartlets. Marsala sauce. Parmesan cheese.
BARIGOULE Carciofi:	Artichokes casseroled with pork, mushrooms, onions & wine.
BASILICO	Sweet basil. A herb — Ocymum basilium.
BAVARESE	Gelatin reinforced custard with whipped cream.
all'Arancia:	With orange.

DINERS' DICTIONARY

al caffe:	Coffee.
al cioccolato:	Chocolate.
alle fragole:	Strawberry.
alle nocciole:	Hazel nuts.
alla vaniglia:	Vanilla.
BAVETTE	A small flat ribbon pasta of which Bavettine is an even smaller form.
alla Trasteverina:	With anchovies, tuna & mushrooms.
BECCACCE-IA	Woodcock.
al fine champagne:	Fried & dissected with brandy on fried bread. Foie gras.
sul crustone:	Whole on toast. Foie gras.
in casseruola alla crema:	In a casserole with brandy & cream.
in salmi:	Reduced to a fine conserve. Served on toast.
in salmi Fernanda:	Using red wine.
sautee allo spumante:	Sautéed with a sparkling white wine.
BECCACCINI	Snipe.
al brandy:	Fried with brandy.
allo spiedo:	On a spit. Entrails on toast.
BECCAFICHI	Literally "figpeckers". A small bird. A warbler.
BEL PAESE	A soft mild cheese originating in Lombardy.
BELLA VISTA	
Astaco fredda in:	Cold lobster in aspic with endive, truffles, vegetables, tarragon & mayonnaise.
Costolette di Vitello:	Veal cutlets cold in aspic with any four seasonal vegetables.
BERRICHONS	Almond meringue biscuits or cookies.
BESCIAMELLE	Béchamel sauce. Simple white sauce.
BIANCHETTI	Whitebait. The young of herring & sprats. Very small fry found in sea or estuaries.

ITALIAN

Bigne di:	Whitebait fritters.
BIETOLE	Chard. Similar to spinach.
BIGNE	Fritters. French "beignets".
di accuighe salate:	Anchovy fritters.
di albicocche:	Apricot fritters with Aurum liqueur.
di bianchetti:	Whitebait fritters.
di camembert:	Camembert cheese fritters.
di cavolfiore:	Cauliflower fritters.
di conchiglie St. Jacques:	Scallop fritters.
di creme rovesciata:	Custard fritters.
di filetti di baccala:	Cod fritters.
all'Italiana:	Chicken, ham, lamb brains, cheese & tomato sauce fritters.
di Lumache con salsa di pomodoro:	Snail fritters with tomatoes.
di melanzane:	Aubergine or egg plant fritters.
di mele con salsa di albicocche:	Apple fritters with apricot sauce.
di ostriche all'Itàliana:	Oyster fritters with tomato sauce.
al parmigiano:	Cheese fritters.
di pesce:	Fish fritters (herring).
di pomodori:	Tomato fritters.
di San Guiseppe:	Fritters of egg, lemon & vanilla. Traditional on St. Joseph's Day (19th March).
di sardine:	Sardine fritters.
di scorzonera:	Salsify fritters.
souffles ripiena di confettura calda:	Jam or cream filled fritters.
BIRRA	Beer.
BISATO	Eels. Cooked over fire.
BISCOTTI-O-INI	Biscuits or cookies.
all'anice:	Aniseed flavored.
Arrotolato:	Apricot roll.
al burro:	Petits fours.

DINERS' DICTIONARY

Comuni:	Sweet & puffed.
di Dama:	With butter & raisins.
di Famiglia:	Orange flower flavored.
al limone:	Lemon flavored.
di Novaro:	With egg & vanilla.
tipo Pavesini:	With egg, vanilla & almond.
BISTECCHE	
al'Amburghese:	Hamburger.
all'Americana:	Raw minced fillet of beef with egg yolk in center. Onions, sauce, brandy, capers.
a Cavallo:	Egg yolks on fried fillet steak.
alla crema:	Minced beef & ham fried. With cream.
alla Fiorentina:	T-bone steak grilled over charcoal.
alla Nizzarda:	Fried minced beef with onions & garlic.
della Nonna:	Minced beef, white sauce, cheese & breadcrumbs.
alla Pizzaiola:	Steak with tomato, garlic & oregano spread over. May be tough! (Naples).
alla tartara:	Raw fillet of beef. Tartare sauce, brandy & Worcester sauce.
BITOKES	
alla russa:	Minced beef, onions, nutmeg & cream. Fried.
BITTO	Cheese made from mixture of cow & goat milk. (Lombardy).
BLANQUETTE	
di vitello all'Antica:	Veal stew with vegetables, herbs & cream.
BLU	
al blu:	The French "au bleu". Trout etc. cooked in boiling stock *immediately* after killing.
BOCCONCINI	Roll of veal & ham with cheese in center. Cooked in butter. Tomato sauce.
BOCCONE SQUADRISTA	A sandwich of fish cutlet between

	apple. Flamed in rum.
BOCCONOTTI	A type of tart.
di ricotta alla Romana:	A cold cheese & fruit tart.
BOGA (BOGHE)	A sea fish.
BOLDRO	Tuscany name for angler fish.
BOLETUS	A type of edible fungus, Funghi procini, which is dried.
BOLLITI-O	Literally "boiled".
Misti:	Mixture of beef, lamb, veal & pork boiled with vegetables. A specialty of Piedmont.
"all'Italiana:	As the above but containing a stuffed capon.
di Famiglia:	Beef boiled with herbs & vegetables. Rice served seperately — usually first.
BOLOGNESE	After town of Bologna.
Baccalla alla:	Strips of dried cod fried with onions, garlic, parsley & pepper.
Fegatelli di Maiale:	Pork liver on skewers alternated with bread cubes & sage.
Fritto:	Fried veal, brains, ham, truffles, cheese & white sauce.
Fritto Misto alla:	As above with veal etc. on skewers (stecchi), lamb chops, liver, chicken & vegetables.
Salsa di:	Ham, onion, celery, carrot, garlic, basil, mushrooms, wine, parsley, marjoram, nutmeg, tomatoes. Called RAGU.
Sauce for pasta:	Beef, chicken liver, ham, carrot, onion, celery, tomato paste, white wine, stock, butter, nutmeg. Proper name RAGU.
Stecchi alla:	Veal, sausage, gruyère cheese & bread on sticks. Deep fried with eggs & crumbs.

DINERS' DICTIONARY

Filette di Tacchino alla:	Turkey breasts fried in crumbs with ham & cheese.
Trippa alla:	Tripe in oil & butter with onion, garlic, parsley, meat sauce, cheese & lean pork.
Tortellini:	Half-moons of pasta stuffed with pork, veal, turkey, ham, brains, cheese, egg & nutmeg.
Medaglioni di Vitello alla:	Small veal steaks fried in crumbs. With ham, cheese & truffles.
BOMBA DI RISO	Oven cooked pigeons with rice. Specialty of Parma.
BOMBOLOTTI	Short smooth cylinders of pasta.
BONDIOLA	Cured shoulder of pork with wine. (Parma).
BONNE MAMAN Animella di vitello:	Veal sweetbreads casseroled with celery, carrots & onions. White wine.
BORDOLESE	Style of Bordeaux. French "Bordelaise".
Astaco alla:	Lobster fried in butter & brandy. Tomato sauce.
BORGHESE	Named from an old noble Italian family.
Lingua di bue:	Ox tongue braised with brandy, herbs, red wine & diced salt pork.
Oca farcita alla:	Roast goose stuffed with onions, apples, chestnuts, pine nuts, allspice, pork, goose liver & brandy.
Ragu di bue alla:	Cut up rump steak stewed with chopped onion, carrot & celery. Herbs.
Trippa alla moda:	Tripe in butter with onion, carrots, mushrooms, garlic, herbs & stock.
BORGOGNONA	In the style of Burgundy. French "Bourguigonne".
Anguilla alla:	Hot or Cold. Pieces of eel in oil, garlic

ITALIAN

	& shallots. Brandy, anchovy butter. As an antipasta.
BORLOTTI BOSCAIOLA Bucatini alla:	Dried red haricot beans. Small tubular pasta with aubergines or egg plant, tomatoes & mushrooms.
BOTTARGA	Smoked fish roe with oil & lemon.
BOVOLONI	Snails.
BRACIOLA— ETTE—INE	Thin slices of meat.
di manzo farcite:	Rump steak thinly sliced, rolled & stuffed with veal, ham, liver & herbs. Boiled with tomatoes.
di manzo farcite alla Napoletana:	As the above but stuffed with nuts, raisins, herbs & garlic.
Ripiene:	Veal rolls stuffed with nuts, cheese & sultanas.
d'agnello al marsala con crocchettine di patate:	Fried sliced lamb with marsala & potato croquettes.
d'agnello con carciofi:	Fried sliced lamb with artichokes.
di vitello con burro piccante:	Fried sliced veal with anchovy butter, garlic, parsley & lemon juice.

DINERS' DICTIONARY

BRACIUOLA	A chop.
BRANZIN—ETTI—O	Bass. This and Dentice are similar sea fish.
alla Casalinga:	Casseroled in wine, butter & onion. Anchovy sauce.
alla Mugnaia con peperoni:	Cooked in butter with roasted peppers.
alla Nizzarda:	Fried with onions, olives, tomatoes & herbs. Anchovy fillets.
arrista:	Roasted. With wine (Bercy) sauce.
freddo conolio e limone:	Cold. Oil & lemon.
alla Ghiottona:	Grilled in wine & herbs & skinned. Tomato & anchovy sauce & carrots.
lessato con salsa Normanda:	Poached with a fish (Normande) sauce.
lessato con salsa Olandese:	Poached with yolk & lemon (Hollandaise) sauce.
BRASATO	Braised or braising.
BRASATURA	Braised or braising.
BRESAOLA	Dried salt beef. Antipasta with oil, lemon juice & parsley. (Lombardy).
BRIDA Filetti di sogliola Fantasaia di:	Sole stewed in a marinade with shrimps, shallots, tomatoes & vermouth. Cream & artichokes.
BRIOSCIA	French "brioche". Cake of yeast-leavened dough.
BROCCOLETTI DI RAPE BROCCOLI RAVE	Like broccoli but very small flower heads
all'agro:	Boiled. Hot or Cold. Vinegar-oil dressing.

ITALIAN

lessati e insaporiti con aglio e olio:	As above but cooked in oil and garlic.
BROCCOLI	Broccoli.
Romani:	Cooked in wine & garlic.
Romani al proscuitto:	As above with chopped ham.
alla Siciliana:	Casseroled with onions, olives, anchovies & Caciocavallo cheese.
BRODETTATO	Small cubes of meat stewed in wine with egg yolks & cheese.
Agnello:	Lamb as above.
BRODETTO	A complex soup.
delle coste Adriatiche:	Of fish. Similar to French "Bouillabaisse" or "Bourride".
alla Maniera di Cattolica:	Similar to the above with shrimps & squid.
alla Romana:	Beef, lamb & herb soup. Traditional at Easter.
BRODO	A clear soup with e.g. the following additions:
Bolognese:	White stock with egg, crumbs & cheese.
con lattughe:	With lettuce.
di magro:	With vegetables.
con pangrattato:	With breadcrumbs.
con passatelli:	With a crumb, egg, cheese & marrow or squash dough like spaghetti.
di pesce:	With fish.
di pesce Ristretto:	Fish consommé.
di pollo:	With chicken.
di pollo Ristretto:	Chicken consommé.
Ristretto:	Simple consommé.
con Uova filate:	With egg, flour & cheese strips.
con vegetable:	With vegetables.
BRUSCHETTA	Crisp oven-baked slices of bread rubbed in garlic & soaked in olive oil.

DINERS' DICTIONARY

BUCATINI	The smallest of the tubular pastas.
con acciughe:	With anchovies. Traditional Naples on Christmas Eve.
alla Boscaiola:	With aubergines or egg plant, tomatoes & mushrooms.
del Buongustaio:	Similar to the above.
alla Domenicana:	With anchovies.
alla Freda:	With sausages & tomatoes.
con cozze e vognole:	With mussels & baby clams.
con salsiccia:	With sausages & tomatoes.
BUDELLI	Offal or variety meats.
BUDINO	Pudding. All the well-known puddings such as cabinet, chocolate, Queens & rice occur with Italian names.
BUE	Ox or beef. See also MANZO.
Bistecca di:	Steak — can be of minced beef.
Brasato con gnocchi:	Braised beef in wine, brandy & herbs with potato dumplings.
Brasato al Ricca:	As the above with onions & mushrooms instead of dumplings.
Costata di:	Ribs.
Filetti di:	Fillet steak — undercut of the sirloin.
alla moda in gelatina:	Cold beef in aspic.
Involtini di:	Thin slices rolled & stuffed.
Lombatines di:	Small steaks from rib end of sirloin. French "entrecôte".
Spalla di:	Shoulder.
Tournedos di:	A steak cut from the eye of the fillet of beef. About 4 ozs; 100 grams.
BUONGUSTAIO	Literally "tasting good".
Bucatini del:	Pasta with aubergines or egg plant, tomatoes & mushrooms.
Coda di bue:	Oxtail stewed with pork, onions, carrots, garlic, cloves & herbs. Oven browned in crumbs.

ITALIAN

Filetti di bue:	Steak fried in mushrooms, truffles & foie gras on fried bread.
Piccioncelli alla:	Squabs spatchcocked (young pigeons split in half) fried in brandy. Chicken & meat stock & parsley.
Fricassea al Rombetto del:	Turbot sliced. In butter with sole, mussels, onions, mushrooms & cream.
BURRIDA	Fish stew. Specialty of Genoa. Similar to French "Bouillabaisse" or "Bourride".
BURRINI	A southern Italian cheese from cows' milk which when cut has fresh butter in the center.
BURRO	Butter. Anchovy, garlic, parsley butter etc. are all given their specific name e.g. garlic butter in Burro d'aglio.
BUSECCA	Soup or stew of vegetables & tripe (ox stomach). (Milan).
BUTIRRI	Alternative name for Burrini cheese.
BUTTARIGA	Eggs of grey mullet eaten with oil & lemon.
BUTTERA	Bacon, celery, basil, onions, mushrooms & chillies in tomato sauce. With pasta.

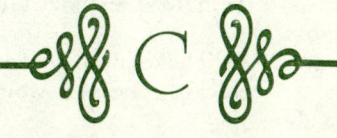

C

CACCIATORO	Literally "hunter".
Agnello alla Cacciatoro con aceto:	Cubes of lamb cooked in oil & rosemary. With garlic, vinegar & anchovy sauce.

	meat, wine, peas, artichokes, mushrooms & cheese.
Salsa:	Sauce for cold fish. Pistachio nuts, pine nuts, white sauce, egg yolks, lemon & herb purée.
Sarde:	Sardines stuffed with cheese, parsley, basil & oregano and fried in crumbs.
Stecchi alla:	Chicken livers, sweetbreads, tongue & gruyère on sticks. Cheese sauce. Crumbed & deep fried.
Stufato di manzo alla:	Stewed beef, onions, tomatoes, carrots, celery & white wine.
Trippa alla:	Tripe. Ham, onions, garlic, wine, parsley, rosemary, tomatoes, cheese & stock. In oil.
GERMANO	Mallard. Wild duck.
GETTONI	Small praline flavored sweets.
GHIOTTE-ONA-ONE	Literally "gourmet or greedy".
Costolettine d'agnello:	Braised lamb chops with onion sauce, courgettes or zucchini & tomato sauce.
Aringhe salate del:	Salt herring fillets with onions, shallots, parsley, basil, celery & mayonnaise.
Branzino alla:	Bass grilled in wine & herbs & skinned. Tomato & anchovy sauce. Carrots.
Fondi di carciofa del:	Artichokes oven cooked with minced chicken, cheese & white sauce.
Costolette di maiale alla:	Pork chops marinaded & casseroled. Mushrooms, garlic, rosemary & parsley.
Funghi freddi alla:	Cold. Mushrooms with shrimps, asparagus, artichokes, truffles, mayonnaise, mustard & Worcester sauce.

ITALIAN

Salsa:	For pasta. Fresh peas & truffles.
GIAMBONETTI	Legs & thighs (of capon).
GIANCHETTI	Tiny boneless white sea fish.
GINEPRO	Juniper berries.
GIODDU	Yogurt. (Sardinia).
GIOVARRO	Chuck of beef.
GIRASOLE	Sunflower. Helianthus annuus. Seed & Oil used
GIRATI	Stirred.
GUIDEA	Jewish.
Carciofi alla:	Artichokes crisply fried in deep oil.
GNOCCHI	Poached dumplings made of flour, cheese & eggs. A Rome specialty is made with potatoes quite different from "Gnocchi di semolina alla Romana" which is made from semolina. Gnocchi verdi has spinach added.
GNOMMARIELLI	Spit roasted baby lamb offal or variety meats.
GORGONZOLA	Cows herbed blue cheese from Lombardy.
GRANA	Literally "granular" Common name of Parmesan cheese.
GRANATINA	"Hamburger".
GRANCE-MIO-OLE-VOLE	Large scarlet spider crabs.
GRANCIPORRO	Common edible crab.
GRAND HOTEL Coppa:	Cup of maraschino ice cream, cherries, curaçao & apricot sauce.

DINERS' DICTIONARY

Nicciole d'agnello alla:	Small lamb steaks with onions, white wine, mushrooms, stock & tomato sauce.
Capretto alla:	Kid stewed in stock, tomatoes, onions, mushrooms & brandy.
Lasagne:	Layers of chicken, pork, garlic, tomatoes, cheese, parsley & wine with sheets-of pasta.
Salsa:	Onions, mushrooms & tomato.
Or	The name of a small salami (250 grams). Little salt & matured for only a short time.
CACCIUCCO delle coste Mediterranee:	Fish stew.
Or Livornese:	With garlic & peppers, as a main dish. Served with oven-baked slices of bread.
CACIO A CAVALLO	A buffalo cheese made in the shape of two saddlebags for a horse.
CALABRESE	Tomato & ginger sauce. With pasta.
CALAMAR— ETTI—I	Squid or inkfish.
con carciofi:	With artichokes.
fritti:	Fried.
gratellati:	Grilled.
Ripieni al forno:	Stuffed & baked.
alla Teglia:	With anchovies in a pie-dish.
in Umido:	Stewed in wine, herbs & some of its own ink.
in Zimino:	With chopped beet leaves. A specialty of Genoa.
CALDA—E—O	Hot.
CALZONE IMBOTTITO	A Nepolitan specialty. Half-moon containers of pizza dough filled with ham & cheese, baked in a hot oven.

ITALIAN

CAMPAGNA	Beef & cheese sauce. With pasta.
CAMPAGNOLA	Anchovies, garlic, red peppers, wine, mushrooms & tomato sauce. With pasta.
CANAPES	Small pieces of bread or toast with a savory preparation. The word is French and means "couch". Cold antipasta. There are many preparations which are self-explanatory e.g. Canapes di acciughe — anchovy canapes.
CANESTRATO	A sheeps cheese from Sicily.
CANESTRELLO	A bi-valve shellfish. Pilgrim scallop.
CANNELINI	White haricot, kidney or navy beans. Seed of Phaseolus vulgaris.
CANELLA	Cinnamon.
CANNELLONI	A pasta case with filling. Includes Ravioli, Tortellini, Cappelletti and Agnolotti. Ravioli and Agnolotti are the same except for the content -Ravioli must contain the soft sheep's cheese, Ricotta & possibly spinach. The contents are named in the title.
CANNOLI ALLA SICILIANA	A pastry filled with Ricotta cheese, fruit & nuts. Fried in deep fat.
CANNOLICCHI	A short tubular pasta.
CANOCHIE	Shrimps.
CANTARELLA	A sea fish. Black bream.
CANTARELLO	Chanterelle. Edible fungus. Cantharellus cibarius.
CAPAROZZOLO	Venice name for small clam. Venus verrucosa.
CAPE SANTE	Scallops. Also called CONCHIGLIA DEI PELLIGRINI.
CAPITONE	Eels.
CAPOCOLLA	Cured shoulder of pork. (Parma).
CAPONATA	Served as a vegetable or cold antipasta. (Sicily). Fried aubergines or egg plant,

DINERS' DICTIONARY

	with capers, olives, celery, anchovies, onions & tomatoes. Vinegar & parsley. With tuna, lobster or tuna eggs.
CAPONATA ALLA MARINARA	Quite different from CAPONATA. Primitive dish. Bread or hard biscuits (cookies) soaked in water with garlic, black olives, anchovies & herbs.
CAPONE	A sea fish. Gurnard. Literally "sea hen". Sea robin.
CAPPA—E	Bi-valve mollusc.
CAPPELLE DI FUNGHI	Mushroom caps.
farcite:	Stuffed.
gratinati:	Browned.
sulla foglia di vite:	With vine leaves.
CAPPELLETI	A form of canelloni (packet of stuffed pasta) shaped like a cocked hat.
con pistacchi:	With pistachio nuts.
al sugo di carne alla Romana:	With turkey, ham, cheese & brain stuffing. With meat, mushroom & herb (Italian) sauce.
CAPPON MAGRO	Fish salad. Specialty of Genoa. Very variable. Hard biscuit (cookie) or bread base. Potatoes, carrots, artichokes, celery, beet, beans, cauliflower & olives, white fish, lobster, shrimp & crab. Oil, vinegar, parsley, garlic (in quantity), eggs, anchovies, herbs & capers. A very filling garlic dish!
CAPPONE	Capon. A castrated cockerel.
in casseruola Angiola Teresa:	Stuffed with parsley. Cream, foie gras, egg, ham & white wine.
in casseruola alla Paesana:	Casseroled with wine, tomatoes, ham,

	courgettes or zucchini & peppers.
farcito lessato con salsa di capperi:	Boiled & stuffed with caper sauce.
Giambonetti di:	Legs & thighs.
lessato al "sale grosso" con salse verde:	Boiled with herb & vinegar sauce. Coarse salt on the side.
CAPPUCCINA	
Baccala alla:	Dried cod flaked & baked. With cheese & potatoes.
Carpio alla:	Carp filleted & oven cooked in crumbs with oregano.
CAPRA – O	Goat.
CAPRESE	Style of Isle of Capri.
Ravioli:	Filled with mixture of cheese, milk, pepper, nutmeg & marjoram or basil.
Zuppa di pesce:	Soup of oil, tomato, white wine, octopus, large shrimps (mazzancolle) & sliced tonnetto (similar to mackerel).
CAPRETTO	Kid. Young goat.
alla Cacciatora:	Cubes of kid stewed in stock, tomato, onion, brandy & mushrooms.
all'Italiana:	Boned, rolled & roasted in crumbs with garlic, rosemary, parsley & wine.
ripieno al forno:	Roasted & stuffed with herbs. Specialty of Calabria.
CAPRICCIOSE	Literally "capricious".
Costolettine d'agnello:	Lamb chops fried & served with fried salt pork, baked tomatoes, mushrooms, garlic & parsley.
Fondi di carciofo:	Artichoke hearts, truffles, foie gras, parsley & wine sauce.
Cozze:	Cold mussels with mayonnaise, mustard & sliced potatoes.
Filetti di bue:	Fillet steak marinaded, fried in crumbs on anchovy toast.

DINERS' DICTIONARY

CAPRIOLA—O	Roe-buck. Deer.
Cosciotto di:	Haunch of venison.
Costolette di:	Venison loin steaks.
CARABINIERA	Literally "policeman".
Acciughe alla:	Salad of anchovies, potatoes, onions & olives. Cold antipasta.
CARAMELLE	Caramel.
Caffe:	Coffee caramel.
Cioccolato:	Chocolate caramel.
CARBONADES	Flemish method of cooking beef in beer.
di bue alla fiamminga:	Casseroled scallops of beef with beer, butter, onions & sugar. Bread browned in fat.
CARBONARA	Spaghetti with bacon, eggs & butter or cream.
CARCIOFI	Globe artichokes.
Animella di vitello con:	Fried veal sweetbreads with artichokes.
Cold Antipasta	
Fondi di carciofi alla Borghese:	Hearts marinated with vegetables.
Fondi di carciofi alla Greca:	Hearts boiled with herbs & fennel.
Fondi di carciofi con purea di tonno:	Cold hearts with mayonnaise & mashed with tuna fish.
As a vegetable	
Barigoule:	Casseroled with pork, mushrooms, onions & wine.
Casalinga:	Casseroled with onion, lettuce & small peas.
Cavour:	Oven cooked with cheese, parsley, eggs & anchovies.
Fiorentina:	Oven cooked with spinach and cheese (Mornay) sauce.
Ghiottone:	Oven cooked with minced chicken,

	cheese and white sauce.
Guidea:	Crisply cooked in very hot deep oil. Rome specialty at Easter.
ripiena alla Mafalda:	Stuffed with crumbs, anchovies & garlic. Wine.
al tegome alla Romana:	Casseroled. Garlic, mint & breadcrumbs.
alla Veneziana:	Small violet artichokes stewed in oil, white wine & water.
CARDI	Cardoons. A vegetable of the thistle family like beet or seakale which is blanched.
CARNE	Meat.
CAROTA—E	Carrot.
CARPIO	Carp. A freshwater fish.
alla Cappuccina:	Filleted, oven cooked in breadcrumbs with oregàno.
CARRE	Rib or loin (of pork).
di Maiale arrostito:	Roast.
di Maiale alla Paesana:	Roast — with garlic, thyme, rosemary, bay leaf, stock & white wine.
CARTOCCIO	Cooked & served in greaseproof paper cases. Al Cartoccio — French "en papillotes".
Costolettine d'agnello al:	Lamb cooked & served in a paper case.
CARVI	Caraway. A herb.
CASA NOSTRA Filetti di sogliola:	Sole in butter with onion, tomato, basil, courgettes or zucchini & crumbs.
CASALINGA	Literally "domestic".
Cosciotto d'Agnello alla:	Roast leg of lamb with potatoes, onions & rosemary.

DINERS' DICTIONARY

Antipasta alla:	Peppers, tomatoes, onions, dressing, fish in oil. Cold.
Branzinette alla:	Bass casseroled in wine, butter & onion. Anchovy sauce.
Carciofi alla:	Artichokes casseroled with onion, lettuce & small peas.
Minestre di fagioli alla:	Soup of haricot beans, tomatoes, herbs and pasta.
Orata:	Sea-beam or Porgy baked with herbs, white wine & anchovies.
Fegato di Vitello alla:	Veal liver sliced & fried with onions.
Petto di Vitello ripieno alla:	Boned breast of veal stuffed with ham, pork, sausage, garlic & parsley.
CASANOVA Filetto:	Fillet steak with brandy, marsala & goose liver.
CASINO Filette di bue:	Fillet steak fried with ham, mushrooms, parsley & wine sauce.
CASO FORTE	A Neopolitan cheese.
CASOEULA (or CAZZUOLA)	Milanese stewed pork. Pork, sausage, bacon with cabbage & other vegetables.
CASSATA	Partly iced cream cake. Chocolate & candied fruit.
CASSERUOLA	Casserole.
CASSOLA	Fish stew. (Sardinia).
CASTAGNE	Chestnuts.
CASTELMAGNO	A strong, salty herbed cheese of Piedmont.

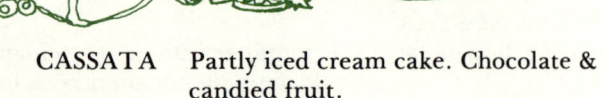

ITALIAN

CASTRADINA	Roast mutton. (Veneto).
CAVALLEGGERA Spaghetti alla:	Pasta with eggs & walnuts.
CAVALLO Bistecche a:	Egg yolks on fried fillet steak.
CAVEDANO	Chub. A freshwater fish.
CAVIALE	Caviar.
CAVIGLIONE	Alternative name for Red Gurnard.
CAVOLFIORE	Cauliflower.
CAVOLINI DI BRUXELLES	Brussel sprouts.
CAVOLI	Cabbage.
CAVOUR Carciofi:	Globe artichokes. Oven cooked with cheese, parsley, eggs & anchovies.
CAZZUOLA (or CASOEULA)	Milanese stewed pork. Pork, sausage, bacon with cabbage & other vegetables.
CECHE-INE	Eels.
CECI	Chick peas. Cicer arietinum. A pea grown in India, Spain, South America & southern U.S.A.
CEFALO	Grey mullet. A sea and harbor fish.
CENA	Supper.
CENCI FIORENTINA	Literally "rays". Traditional of Florence or Rome. Thin slivers of dough fried. Sugar & custard.
CERFOGLIO	Chervil. A European annual herb like parsley.
CERIGNOLA	Very large green olives. (Apulia).
CERNIA	Seafish. Grouper. French "Merou".
CERVELLA-O	Brains. Usually of veal — Cervello di vitello.
CERVO	Deer.
CESTINI	Small pastry cases with savory filling.
CETRIOLINI	Cucumber.

DINERS' DICTIONARY

CHALLAH	Jewish sabbath bread.
CHENELLE	Dumplings e.g. of semolina.
CHENELLINE	Small dumplings of forcemeat or fish. French "quenelles".
CHIOCCOLE	Snails. OR Pasta shaped like snail shells. Important to know which you are getting!
CHIODO DI GAROFANO	Cloves. "Chiodo" — literally "nail".
CHIZZA	Crisp pastry often with cheese.
CHOUX	Cream puffs.
CIALDE	Waffles.
CICALA DI MARE	Shrimps.
CICCIOLI	Sausage for frying.
CICOREA-I	Chicory.
CILIEGE	Cherries.
Barchette con:	Sour cherry & almond tartlets.
Costolette di capriolo con:	Venison steaks with cherries.
CIMA	Specialty of Genoa. Poached veal, cold & stuffed with pork, cheese, turnips, peas, sweetbreads, brains, nuts, eggs, artichokes & marjoram.
CINGHIALE	Wild boar.
CIOCCOLATO	Chocolate.
CIPOLLE	Onions.
CIPOLLINE	White onions or chives.
CIUPIN	Fish stew.
CLAVIARI	Type of mushroom.
COCOMERO	Water melon.
CODA DI BUE	Oxtail. Coda = tail.
del Buongustaio:	After stewing with pork, onions, carrots, garlic, cloves & herbs, oven browned in crumbs.
all'Italiana:	Stewed with vegetables, herbs, garlic, mushrooms, white wine, tomatoes, sausages & celery.

ITALIAN

alla Vacciniera:	Stewed with vegetables, stock, herbs, wine, tomatoes, pine nuts & raisins.
COLAZIONI	Meal.
COLLO	Collar (of lamb, mutton or beef).
COLOMBI	Pigeons.
COMPOSTA	French "compôte". Fresh or dried fruit poached in syrup. Served ice cold.
CONCHIGLIE	Shells.
di astaco "Tirli in Birli":	Lobster hot in scallop shells with onions, mushrooms, eggs & truffles.
di ostriche al curry:	Curried oysters served in the bottom shells.
di pollo all'Italiana:	Chicken, mushrooms & potatoes served hot in scallop shells.
di scampi "Lucullo":	Large shrimps with mushrooms & cheese sauce in scallop shells.
St. Jacques:	Scallops. Most recipes are standard French names.
CONDE Albicocche:	Apricot condé. A hot sweet of apricots with creamed rice.
CONIGLIO	Rabbit. Usually casseroled, fried or stewed in cream.
CONSOMME	Concentrated clear soup, hot, cold or jellied. May contain tapioca. Do *NOT* add parmesan.
CONTADINA Acciughe alla:	Cold. Anchovies with parsley, capers & onions. Olives.
Fegato di vitello alla:	Sliced veal liver fried with onions & garlic.
Insalata:	Salad of potatoes, green beans, black-eyed beans, onion, tomatoes & basil.

DINERS' DICTIONARY

Minestre di ceci alla:	Soup of chick peas, endive, ham, tomatoes & cheese. Bread.
Orata:	Sea bream or Porgy casseroled with herbs, wine, onion & tomatoes.
Sarde alla:	Sardines fried with tomatoes, garlic, parsley & basil.
CONTI Costolette di capriolo:	Venison steaks with lentil purée.
CONTROFILETTO di bue alla mainera del maestro:	Sirloin steak. Marinaded & oven cooked. Onion & marinade sauce. Creamed mushrooms.
di bue Primaverile:	With ham & salt pork. Marinaded & oven cooked. Green beans & potatoes.
COPATE	Sweet wafer-like cakes.
COPPA	Cured shoulder of pork (Parma).
Or	Pig's head brawn (Rome).
Or	Meat loaf of ham, tongue & sausage (Veneto).
Or	French "coupe". One or more types of ice cream or water ice in a cup or glass with fruit, cream or other ingredients:
Dama Bianca:	Almond ice cream, pears, currant jelly, lemon ice.
Deliziosa:	Apricot compôte, kirsch, almonds, apricot ice cream.
Grand Hotel:	Maraschino ice cream, cherries, curaçao, apricot sauce.
Jacques:	Strawberries, raspberries, peaches, apples, cherries, lemon ice, strawberry ice, almonds.
Maria Teresa:	Peach compôte, Drambuie, peach ice cream, almonds.
CORATELLA	Pluck i.e. lungs, heart & liver.
CORDULAS	Sheep offal or variety meats on skewers.
COREGONE	Lake fish.

ITALIAN

COSCE DE RANE	Frogs legs.
COSCETTO	Leg (of mutton).
COSCIOTTO	Leg or haunch (of lamb, mutton, venison or suckling pig).
d'agnello all'Abruzzese:	Leg of lamb braised with rosemary, garlic, white wine & tomatoes.
d'agnello all'Aretina:	Leg of lamb roasted with garlic & red wine & rosemary marinade.
d'agnello arrosto:	Roast leg of lamb.
d'agnello Casalinga:	Roast leg of lamb with potatoes, onions & rosemary.
d'agnello all'Inglese:	Boiled leg of lamb. Turnips, carrots, onions & milk, yolk & lemon (Bastard) sauce.
d'agnello Pasquale:	Marinaded ham inserted into slits of a leg of lamb & braised in white wine.
COSTA DI MAIALE	Pork chop.
COSTATA	Rib (of beef).
di bue arrostita:	Roast rib of beef.
di bue casseruola:	Casseroled rib of beef.
di bue alla Luigi Veronelli:	Rib of beef marinaded, oven cooked with mushrooms.
di bue alla Pizzaiola:	Sliced rib of beef with pizzaiola sauce.
di bue con Primizie:	Roast rib of beef with carrots, green beans, artichokes & peas.
COSTOLETTE-INE D'ANGELLO	Rib chops of lamb or mutton.
Capricciose:	Fried & served with fried salt pork, baked tomatoes, mushrooms, garlic & parsley.

DINERS' DICTIONARY

Cartoccio:	Cooked & served in paper case.
alla Finanziera:	With madeira & truffle (Finanziera) sauce.
Ghiotte:	Braised. Onion sauce, courgettes or zucchini & tomato sauce.
alla Villeroy:	With yolk, ham & truffle (Villeroy) & tomato sauces.

COSTOLETTE DI CAPRIOLO — Venison loin steaks.

con ciliege:	With cherries.
Conti:	With lentil purée.
alla crema:	With cream.
al Ginepro:	With juniper berries.
con testine di funghi:	With mushroom caps.

COSTOLETTE DI MAIALE — Pork chops.

alla Ghiottona:	Marinaded & casseroled with mushrooms, garlic, rosemary & parsley.
Modenese:	In wine, rosemary, sage & garlic.
Napoletana:	In garlic, peppers, tomatoes & mushrooms.
Piccanti:	With onion, garlic, wine, dill pickles & Worcester sauce.
Rafano:	With radish sauce.

COSTOLETTE DI POLLO — Breast of chicken (filetti) with wing attached. For recipes see FILETTI DI POLLO.

COSTOLETTE DI VITELLO — Veal cutlets or chops.

Bella Vista:	Cold in aspic with any four seasonal vegetables.
Griglia:	Grilled.
Maria Teresa:	Fried in crumbs. Cheese, tomatoes & anchovies.
Milanese:	In breadcrumbs & cheese.

ITALIAN

Paesana:	Casseroled with carrots, leeks, onions, celery & potatoes.
Veronelli:	In crumbs. Wine, onions, garlic, ham & herbs.
COTECHINO	A sausage from pork, bay leaf, thyme, sage & vanilla.
COTENNE DI MAIALE	Pork rind. Served stewed with beans.
COZZE	Mussels. Served in French ways e.g. Marinière but also:
all'Ammiraglia:	On skewers with bacon.
Capricciose:	Cold. Mayonnaise, mustard & sliced potato.
alla crema:	Hot in cream.
Ninfetta:	Fried with Worcester sauce.
alla Parigina:	Boiled in wine, shallots & thyme.
Provenzale:	Oven roasted with minced snails.
Ravigotta:	Cold with thick herb sauce. French "ravigote".
Zafferan:	Cold with saffron, tomato, onion & wine sauce.
CREMA	Cream OR cream soups. The contents are named e.g. Cream of artichoke soup — Crema di carciofa etc.
CREMA AL BURRO	Butter cream for cakes.
CREMA INGLESE	Custard with raspberry purée & maraschino.
CRESCENZA	Cow cheese. Creamy yellow. Only available in winter. (Lombardy).
CRESCIONE	Watercress.
CRESPELLE	Thin pancakes or crêpes. Most of the recipes are French.
CRESPONE	Salame (Milano). Equal portions of lean pork, beef & pork fat. Pepper, garlic & white wine. Grainy rice-liked appearance to the fat.
CRISPELLE	Bread or pizza dough fried in hot oil.

DINERS' DICTIONARY

CROCCANTE	Praline. Almonds, vanilla & sugar.
CROCHETTES	Croquettes. A ball of vegetables (rice or potatoes), very fine meat or fish in a thick sauce, egg, crumbed & fried crisp. The name is explanatory e.g. Crochettes di Cozze — Mussel croquettes.
CROQUEMBOUCHE	A complicated and impressive dessert. Cream puffs, cream, chocolate, caramel, pineapple, strawberries & nuts.
CROSTACEA	Crustaceans generally.
CROSTATE	Pie or tart as a first course.
Salate alla Genovese:	Traditional of Genoa. Beet tops, cheese & marjoram.
Salate Capricciosa:	Ham & cheese.
Salate di code di scampi:	Large shrimp tails.
Salate Italiana di fontina:	Fontina cheese.
Salate alla moda di Borgogna:	Italian "quiche lorraine". Bacon & cheese.
Salate Regence:	Mushrooms, chicken livers & madeira.
CROSTE	Crustless squares of fresh bread hollowed & filled, deep fried or oven browned. French "canâpes". Filled with brains, cheese, chicken liver etc. e.g. Croste al formaggio — cheese filled.
CROSTINI	Stale bread trimmed & fried with savory spread on. French "croûte". Cheese, seafood, truffles etc. e.g. Crostini con Gorgonzola.
di Fegatini:	With chicken livers. (Tuscany). (Umbria).

ITALIAN

CRUSTONE	Toast.
Beccaccia sul crustone:	Woodcock on toast.
CULATELLO	Ham. (Parma).
CUNDIUM	Green salad with fish.
CUORE-I	Heart.
CUSCUSU	Pellets of semolina specially prepared & served with casseroled meat or chicken with a hot spicy sauce. Rarely with fish. Cous cous.
CUTTURIDDI	Lamb stewed with rosemary.

D

DADOLATA	French "salpicon". Diced cooked meat or other ingredient used as a garnish.
DAMA BIANCA	French "Dame Blanche".
Coppa:	Cup of almond ice cream, pears, currant jelly & lemon ice.
DAME	Small cakes.
DARNE	French "darne". A thick middle cut of fish such as salmon, thinner than French "tronçon".
DATTERI	Dates.
DATTERI DI MARE	Ligurian shellfish.
DELIZIE ALL 'AMERICANA	A savory of toast with flour, milk, yolk & lemon (Bastard) sauce with anchovy paste & capers.
DELIZIOSA Coppa:	Cup of apricot compôte, kirsch, almonds & apricot ice cream.

DINERS' DICTIONARY

DENTE	Literally "teeth". The phrase "al dente" meaning slightly firm to the bite, referring to pasta.
DENTICE	Mediterranean fish similar to bass. Served as bass — see BRANZINO.
DIANA Fondi di carciofo alla:	Artichokes with sweetbreads, wine, eggs, cheese & white sauce.
DIAVOLINI	Soup garnish. Small rounds of bread, white sauce, cheese & pepper oven browned.
DIAVOLO	French "diable".
Astaco alla:	Lobster oven cooked in mustard sauce.
Salsa:	Wine, vinegar, onion, thyme, tabasco, pepper, cayenne & parsley.
Animello di Vitello:	Veal sweetbreads with tomatoes & wine & pepper sauce.
DIPLOMATICI	Eclairs with Alkermes liqueur.
DOLCI	Sweets, puddings, cakes.
DORATE-O	Golden brown in breadcrumbs.
Baccala fritto:	Pieces of dried cod fried in batter in deep oil. Lemon & parsley.
Alette di Tacchino:	Turkey wings fried. In breadcrumbs.
DORATINI	Cheese fritters.
DORATURA	Browning. Way of finishing fish in oven just before serving.
DORSO DI LEPRE	Fillet of hare from back.
DRAGONCELLO	Tarragon. A herb. Artemisia dracunculus.

E

ECLAIRS	Eclairs. A small finger shaped pastry with cream or other filling.
ELABORATI DI FORMAGGI	Complex cheese mixtures for bread, crackers or biscuits.
ENTRECOTE	A French word used in Italian. The proper Italian word is LOMBATA or LOMBATINE. Top part of sirloin or ribs of beef.
ERBA CIPOLLINA	Chives.
ESTRAGONE	Tarragon. A herb. Artemesia dracunculus.
EVA Banane desiderio di:	Oven cooked bananas with rum, maraschino, Aurum liqueur & cream. Almond macaroons.

F

FABRIANO	A salame which is a mixture of pork & veal.
FAGIANO	Pheasant.
all'Americana:	Grilled spatchcock (split in half) in breadcrumbs with parsley butter, mushrooms & tomatoes.

DINERS' DICTIONARY

arrosto sul crustone:	On toast.
alla belga:	Roasted & casseroled with wine & endive.
in casseruola "Conte di Savoia":	Foie gras & paprika between skin & flesh. Roasted.
in casseruola alla crema:	In cream.
in casseruola alla crema acida enrica:	With cream, lemon juice & mushrooms.
alla griglia:	Grilled.
alla Normanda:	Roasted with apples, Calvados (apple brandy) & cream.
FAGIOLI	
Bianco:	Dried white haricot beans. Seeds of Phaseolus vulgaris when ripe. Also called white kidney or navy beans.
Borlotti:	Dried red haricot beans. A variety of the above. Sometimes called red kidney or cranberry beans.
Toscanelli:	Dried black-eyed beans.
Cannellini:	Small dried white haricot beans as above.
Verdi:	Pods of young french or green beans eaten whole. Phaseolus vulgaris. The runner or string bean Phaseolus multiflorus and the Lima bean Phaseolus lunatus are seldom found in Italy.
FAINA	Thin pancake from chick-pea flour fried in oil. (Sardinia, Piedmont, Genoa).
FAMIGLIA	Literally "of the family".
Bollito di:	Beef boiled with herbs & vegetables. Rice served separately — usually first.
FAMIGLIOLE	A red-topped fungus of Tuscany.

ITALIAN

FANTASIA
Antipasto: Oysters, shrimps, cream, mayonnaise, sherry, lemon. Celery.

Canape: Canapé of fish or crab, mayonnaise & capers.

Filetti di solgiola
Fantasia di Brida: Sole stewed in a marinade with shrimps shallots, tomatoes & vermouth. Cream & artichokes.

Orata: Sea bream or Porgy baked in foil with anchovies.

Salsa: Sauce for cold fish. Oil, egg yolk, mustard, lemon juice, basil, shallots, egg white, Worcester sauce.

FARAONA Guinea fowl. French "pintade-au",

FARCIA Stuffed eggs. With ham, chicken, salmon etc. Cold with mayonnaise e.g. Farcia di gamberetti — Shrimp stuffed eggs.

FARCITA-E Stuffed.

Braciola di manzo: Thinly sliced rump steak rolled & stuffed with veal, ham, liver & herbs. Boiled with tomatoes.

Braciola di manzo alla Napoletana: As above but stuffed with nuts, raisins, herbs & garlic.

FARFALLE Pasta shaped like small butterflies.

FARSUMAGRU Stewed rolled veal stuffed with eggs, cheese & spices. Tomato sauce.

FASOEIL AL FURN Red haricot beans cooked very slowly with pork rind or bacon, parsley, garlic, pepper, cinnamon, cloves & mace.

FATTORE Literally "the agent".

Anguilla alla moda del: Eels fried in breadcrumbs. Mustard sauce.

DINERS' DICTIONARY

FAVE	Broad or shell beans. Vicia faba. Eaten young as seeds or very young in pods. Eaten raw as an antipasta.
al Guaciale:	with chopped onion & bacon. Roman dish.
FEGATELLI di maiale	Pork liver on skewers.
Bolognese:	Marinaded in herbs & alternated with bread cubes & sage leaves.
di maiale Finocchio:	With fennel & alternated with bay leaves.
di maiale Fiorentina:	With garlic & fennel & alternated with bay leaves.
FEGATINI DI POLLO	Chicken livers.
FEGATO	Liver.
di maiale:	Pig liver.
d'oca:	Goose liver.
di vitello:	Veal liver.
di vitello alla Borghese:	Marinaded in brandy. Casseroled with onions & carrots. Wine sauce.
di vitello alla Casalinga:	Sliced & fried with onions.
di vitello alla Contadino:	Sliced & fried with onions & garlic.
di vitello all'Inglese:	Fried with bacon.
di vitello alla Milanese:	Sliced, marinaded & fried in crumbs.
di vitello alla Veneziana:	Thin strips fried. Onions.
FELINO	A village near Parma famous for its irregularly shaped Salame of pure pork, white wine, garlic & pepper.

ITALIAN

FERNET BRANCA	A herb based Italian liqueur with, to put it politely, an acquired taste. Good for stomach upsets & hangovers!
FERRI	Grilled.
FESA PRIMAVERILE	Leg of veal. (Parma).
FETTA	Salty white cheese. (Sardinia).
FETTE	Can mean a slice, cut or rasher-usually of meat.
di salmone:	Salmon steak.
FETTINE DI MAIALE	Pork cutlets.
FETTINE DI PROSCUITTO	Pork cutlets.
FETTUCINE	Ribbon-like pasta slightly larger than Tagliatelle.
FIAMMINGA	Flemish style. French "flamande".
Anguilla fresca alla:	Eels hot or cold. Pieces fried with sorrel, watercress & herbs. Egg yolk, cream & white wine. As an antipasta.
Aspergi:	Asparagus with butter & hard boiled eggs.
Carbonades di bue alla:	Casseroled scallops of beef with beer, butter, onions & sugar. Bread browned in fat.
FICO (FICHI)	Figs.
FILETTI DI BUE	Fillet steak — undercut of the sirloin.
brasata alla Frascate:	Casseroled with pork, onion & carrots. Foie gras, truffles, mushrooms & asparagus.
dell Buongustaio:	Fried with mushrooms, truffles & foie gras on fried bread.
Capricciosi:	Marinaded. Fried in crumbs.

	On anchovy toast.
Casanova:	Grilled with brandy, marsala & goose liver.
Casino:	Fried with ham, mushroom, parsley & wine sauce.
Grand Hotel:	Fried. With courgettes or zucchini, tomatoes, olives, small potatoes & meat sauce.
all'Italiana:	Fried with truffles, cheese & ham.
FILETTI DI MAIALE	Fillet of pork.
FILETTI DI POLLO	Breast of chicken. Many recipes. See also POLLO.
Sotto la Campana:	Fried with mushrooms & cream. Served under small glass bowls.
FILETTI DI SOGLIOLA	Fillet of sole. For recipes see also — SOGLIOLA.
Casa Nostra:	In butter with onion, tomato, basil, courgettes or zucchini & crumbs.
Fantasia di Brida:	Stewed in marinade with shrimps, vermouth, shallots, tomato. Cream & artichokes.
Fantasia Marina:	Fried. Mussels & shrimps. Truffles & whisky.
alla Fiorentina:	Grilled with spinach & cheese sauce.
Maria Teresa:	Baked with mushrooms, shallots & wine. Cream & egg sauce.
FILETTI DI TACCHINO	Breast of turkey.
alla Bolognese:	Fried in breadcrumbs with ham & cheese.
alla Luigi Veronelli:	Oven cooked, wrapped in pancakes & fried in crumbs. Flamed in brandy.
alla Piemontese:	Fried in crumbs with cheese & truffles.
Villa Sassi:	Roasted & chopped. Mixed with

ITALIAN

	onions, sage, mushrooms, eggs. Rolled in ham & baked. On toast. Wine sauce.
FILOTROTTAS	Eels cooked over charcoal on skewers. (Sardinia).
FINANZIERA	In French "financière".
Costolettine d'agnello alla:	Lamb chops with finanziera sauce.
Salsa:	Sauce with vol-au-vents, chicken or meat. Of madeira, meat glaze, truffles, sweetbreads & mushrooms.
FINOCCHI	Fennel. A vegetable similar to celery. The hearts can be served cold as antipasta e.g. Cuori di finocchi alla Greca.
FINOCCHIONA TOSCANA	Tuscany pure pork salami with fennel.
FIOCHETTI	Pasta shaped like small bows.
FIOR D'ALPE	Cow milk buttery cheese without holes.
FIORE MOLLE	Soft bright yellow cheese. (Rome).
FIORENTINA	Style of Florence.
Arista:	Pork roasted in water with garlic & rosemary.
Baccala alla:	Dried cod fried in oil with garlic. Tomato sauce.
Bistecca:	T-bone steak grilled on charcoal.
Fondi di Carciofo alla:	Oven cooked artichokes with spinach and cheese (Mornay) sauce.
Fegatelli di maiale:	Pig liver on skewers with garlic, fennel & bay leaves.
Filetti di sogliola:	Grilled fillet of sole with spinach & cheese (Mornay) sauce.
Fritto Misto di:	Chicken, brains, sweetbread, artichokes & cheese fried.
FISCHIETTI	Literally "small whistle". The smallest of the tubular pasta.

DINERS' DICTIONARY

FLAN	Flan. Open tart or pie. May have savory or sweet filling.
FOCACCIA	Genoese type of bread or pizza made with oil & salt. Eaten with cheese.
di vitello:	Meat balls.
FOGLIA	Leaves.
FOGLIA DI VITE	Vine leaves.
Cappelle di funghi ovoli sulla:	Mushrooms on vine leaves.
FOIOLO IN UMIDO	Tripe stewed with garlic & white wine. (Milan).
FONDANTI	Small croquettes. Small ball of ingredient in egg & crumbs and fried. Vegetables, meat or fish.
FONDI DI CARCIOFO	Artichoke hearts.
FONDUTA	Melted fontina cheese.
Piemontese:	Cheese, milk & egg melted on toast.
FONTINA	White or yellow cheese of Piedmont. Like a rich creamy gruyère.
FORMAGGIO	Cheese — in general.
FORMAGGIO FIORE	Solid cheese of Sardinia. A pecorino (a sheeps cheese). Lasts three months.
FORNO	Oven.
Abbachio al:	Roast baby lamb.
FRAGOLE-INE	Strawberries.
FRAGOLE DI BOSCA	Wild strawberries.

ITALIAN

FRAGOLINE DI MARE	Very small squid or inkfish.
FRASCATI Filetti di bue brasata alla:	Fillet steak casseroled with pork, onion & carrots. Foie gras, truffles, mushrooms & asparagus.
FRATE	Fried.
FREDA Bucatina alla:	Pasta with salsiccia (sausage).
FREDDA-I-O	Cold.
FRESCA	Fresh.
FRITTATA	Omelettes. In all varieties.
Savoiarda:	With pork, potatoes, leeks, parsley & cheese.
FRITTATINE IMBOTTITE	Stuffed pancakes.
FRITTELLE	Fritters.
di polenta alla Lodigiana:	Polenta fried in egg & crumbs with tomato sauce.
di riso:	Rice fritters.
FRITTO	Fried dishes. MISTO means mixed and is more complicated.
alla Bolognese:	Veal, brains, ham, truffles, cheese & white sauce. MISTO may contain meat on skewers, lamb chop, liver, chicken, artichokes & cauliflower also.
Fiorentina:	Chicken, brains, sweetbreads, artichokes & cheese.
Milanese:	MISTO: Veal, sweetbreads, cockscombs & vegetables.
Misto di mare:	Mixed fried fish. Red mullet or goatfish, squid & shrimps.
Piemontese:	A simple pasta-like mixture fried.
Romana:	Chicken meat, tongue & cheese sauce. MISTO: Brains, sweetbreads, kidneys & vegetables.

DINERS' DICTIONARY

FRITTURA	Fried. e.g. Frittura di bianchetti — fried whitebait.
FRUTTA	Fruit.
FRUTTI DI MARE	French "fruits de mer". Shellfish — uni or bivalve. Possibly with crustaceans.
FUNGHI	Mushrooms.
freshi:	Field mushrooms.
ovuli:	Amanita caesarea. Orange.
porcini:	Boletus edulis.
di Serra:	Cultivated mushrooms.
freddi alla Ghiottona:	Cold. With shrimps, asparagus, artichokes, truffles, mayonnaise, mustard & Worcester sauce.
alla Luigi Veronelli:	Hot. Onions, garlic, tomatoes, vinegar. Fried.

G

GALLETTO	Chanterelle. Rubbery yellow fungus — Cantharellus cibarius.
GALLINA	Chicken.
GALLINACCIO	Turkey.
Or	Rubbery yellow fungus — Cantharellus cibarius. Chanterelle.
GALLINELLA	Small sea fish. "Sea hen."
GAMBA	Topside or brisket of beef.
GAMBERETTI	Shrimps.
GAMBERI-O	Freshwater crayfish or seawater shrimps.
GARAFANO	Cloves.
GAROFOLATO	Clove flavored.

ITALIAN

GATTUCIO	Dogfish.
GAUFRES	Waffles.
GELATI-O	Water-ice or cream. French "sorbet". In many varieties.
GELATINA-E	A crystal-clear fruit preparation as a delicate sweet course.
GENOISE AL PARIGIANO	A cheese pasta garnish for clear soups.
GENOVESE	Style of Genoa.
Antipasto alla:	Young raw broad or shell beans, salami & Sardo (a cheese).
Cima:	Stuffed cold veal. Stuffing of pork, cheese, turnips, peas, sweetbreads, brains, nuts, eggs, artichokes & marjoram.
Frittata:	Spinach & cheese omelette.
Funghi alla:	Oven baked mushrooms in oil & vine leaves.
Minestre:	Soup from Cima broth (see above), marjoram, eggs, cheese & pasta.
Minestrone:	Soup of pesto (see below), spinach, beet greens, broad or shell beans, cabbage, potatoes, onions, leeks & pasta.
Moscardini:	Small octopus. In strips & stewed in oil with mushrooms, herbs, onions & tomatoes. Croûtons.
Pesches ripiena alla:	Peaches stuffed with peach, brandy & macaroons. Vanilla wafers. Baked. Warm.
Pesto:	Addition for pastas, soups, fish etc. Blend of basil, spinach, parsley, marjoram, pine nuts, garlic, parmesan & pecorino cheeses, oil & butter.
Ravioli:	Stuffed with beet greens, spinach, chicken, sausage, ham fat. Cheese.
Risotto:	Rice with meat sauce, onion, sausage

DINERS' DICTIONARY

Filetti di bue:	Fried fillet steak. Courgettes or zucchini, tomatoes, olives, small potatoes & meat sauce.
GRANERESI	Sauce for pasta. Walnuts, cheese & garlic.
GRANIT-A-E	Sweetened fruit purées frozen until granular.
GRAPPA	Distilled grape spirit. Vaguely like brandy. With herbs. (Rue).
GRATELLA	Grilled (meat).
GRATICOLA	Charcoal grilled.
GRATINATO	Oven cooked with oil, garlic, herbs & crumbs (fish).
GRATINATURE	French "au gratin". Covering of breadcrumbs or cheese lightly browned in a hot oven.
GRATIUM CARTUSIA	A liqueur from Pavia near Milan. Not exported.
GREMOLATA	Chopped parsley, garlic & lemon peel. A garnish for Osso Buco.
GRENADINE	Small steaks (of veal).
GRIFOLE	Dark grey hard edible fungus or a yellow soft one.
GRIGLIA	Grilled or braised.
GRILLETTATO	Grilled or braised.
GRISSINI	Bread sticks.
GRIVE	French for "thrush". In Sardinia covers Thrush, Fieldfare, Blackbird etc. preserved & served cold.
GRONGO	Conger eel.
GROPETTI	Slice of veal rolled, with ham or other stuffing.
GROVIERA	Cheese — Gruyère.
GUACIALE Fave al:	Broad or shell beans with chopped onion & bacon. Roman dish.

ITALIAN

GUARNIZIONE	Garnish but usually referring to a cold egg salad e.g. Guarnizione di sedani — Celery, egg & vinaigrette.
GUAZZETTO	Hash.
Anguilla in Guazzetto con peperoni e cepolline:	Eels mixed with yellow peppers & white onions.
Baccala in Guazzetto alla Romana:	Dried cod cooked in oil & garlic. Tomatoes, raisins & pine nuts.
GUSCI DI MERINGA	Meringue shells.

IJ

IMBOTTITE	Stuffed.
INDIVIA	Endives or chicory. Usually eaten raw in salad. Can be braised. Usually blanched. Cichorium endivia or intybus.
INFIAMMATI	Flamed. French "flambéd".
INGLESE	Literally "English style".
Cosciotto d'agnello all':	Boiled leg of lamb. Turnips, carrots & onions. Milk, yolk & lemon (Bastard) sauce.
Barbabietole all':	Boiled beet.
Fegato di vitello all':	Fried liver & bacon.
INSALATA	Salad.
Composta:	Mixed.

DINERS' DICTIONARY

Contadina:	New potatoes, green beans, black-eyed beans, onions, tomatoes & basil.
Cotta:	Cold cooked vegetables.
Genovese:	Young raw broad or shell beans, salami & Sardo (a cheese).
Ghiottona:	Endives, shallots, salt pork & vinaigrette.
Maria Teresa:	Celeriac, lettuce, eggs, chicken, truffles, mayonnaise & vinaigrette.
Napoletana:	Cauliflower head, anchovies, olives, capers & eggs.
Nizzarda:	Green beans, potatoes, tomatoes, capers, olives & anchovies.
Siciliana:	Tomatoes, mushrooms, pickles, celery, green beans, anchovies, capers, mayonnaise & vinaigrette.
Stagione:	In season.

INTERIORA	Meat offal or variety meats.
INTINGOLO	Cut into pieces.
di anitra all'Italiana:	Cut duck fried & stewed with onion, celery, carrots, herbs & stock. Fried bread.
di maiale e uccelletti alla Toscana:	Stewed pork rind & tails with grilled spatchcock (split in half) songbirds.
d'oca sual crostone:	Goose stewed with its blood. Served on toast.
INVOLTINI	Thin slices of meat rolled & stuffed. Beef, veal or pork.
ITALIANA	Italian style.

ITALIAN

Nocciole d'agnello all':	Small fried lamb steaks with fried bread, fried ham & white wine sauce.
Ananasso all':	Cold pineapple. Kirsch & strawberry ice.
Aspergi all':	Asparagus with cheese & nut butter.
Bigne all':	Chicken, ham, lamb brains & tomato fritters.
Bigne di ostriche all':	Oyster fritters with tomato sauce.
Bolliti misti all':	Stew of beef, veal, lamb, pork & stuffed capon with vegetables.
Canapes all':	Butter, salami & hard boiled egg canapes.
Capretto all':	Kid boned, rolled & roasted in crumbs with garlic, rosemary, parsley & wine.
Coda di bue all':	Oxtail with vegetables, herbs, garlic, mushrooms, white wine, tomatoes & celery.
Conchiglie di pollo all':	Chicken, mushrooms & potatoes served hot in scallop shells.
Filetti di bue all':	Fillet steak fried with truffles, cheese & ham.
Intingolo di anitra all':	Cut duck fried & stewed with onion, celery, carrots, herbs & stock. Fried bread.
Lasagne all':	Layers of Bolognese sauce, mushrooms & cheese with sheets of pasta.
Melanzane farcite all':	Aubergines or egg plant stuffed with onions, tomatoes & garlic. Baked.
Minestrone all':	Soup of beet greens, pork, onions, ham, haricot beans, courgettes or zucchini & pasta.
Orata all':	Sea bream of Porgy sliced. In vermouth, mushrooms & cream.

DINERS' DICTIONARY

Rombetto farcito all':	Turbot filleted, stuffed & baked. Lobster sauce.
Tartelette all':	Small tarts filled with tomato sauce, wine, ham, tongue, mushrooms & cheese.
Trotelle all':	Trout baked with fennel & white wine.
JACQUES Coppa:	Cup of strawberries, raspberries, peaches, apples, cherries, lemon ice, strawberry ice & almonds.

L

LACCETT	Sweetbreads.
LACERTO	Mackerel.
LAMPONI	Raspberries.
LAPACENDRO BUONO	Edible fungus. Orange milk cap. Lactarius deliciosa.
LASAGNE	The largest of the flat ribbon-like pastas. VERDI — green is made with spinach.
Cacciatoro:	With layers of chicken, pork, garlic, tomatoes, cheese, parsley & wine.
alla Napolitana:	Traditional Naples on Shrove Tuesday. With layers of cheese & ham braised in marsala.
Pasticciata all'Italiana:	With layers of Bolognese sauce, mushrooms & cheese.
alla Piemontese:	With layers of meat sauce, truffles & cheese.

ITALIAN

LASAGNETTE	Slightly smaller than lasagne.
del Lucchese:	With ricotta cheese & chicken livers.
LATTE	Milk.
LATTE DI MANDORLE	Almond milk.
LATTUGHE	Lettuce.
LECCIA	Mackerel.
LEGUMI	Green vegetables.
LENTICCHIE	Lentils.
LEPRE	Hare.
in Agrodolce:	Hare in sweet-sour sauce.
alla Montanura:	Hare stewed with pine nuts & sultanas. (Trento & Veneto).
di Cephalonia:	Marinaded in lemon juice, covered pot cooked in oil, onion, garlic, oregano & red wine.
LESSATURA	Poached.
LESSO-ATO	Boiled. As in Manzo lesso — boiled beef.
LIEVITO	Yeast.
"LILY" Albicocche deliziose:	Cold. Apricots with almonds, orange juice & chocolate.
LIMONE	Lemon.
LINGUA	Tongue. Usually braised (BRASATA).
di bue:	Ox tongue.
di vitello:	Calf's tongue.
LINGUE ALGERINE	Literally "Algerian tongues". A savory. Aubergines or egg plant, cream, flour, eggs, cheese. Fried.
LINGUINE	A quite small flat ribbon-like pasta.
alla aglio e olio:	With garlic & oil. (Campania).
alla Luigi Veronelli:	With clams, mussels, shrimps, squid, white wine, onion & garlic. Tomatoes, tuna fish, anchovy butter & parsley.

DINERS' DICTIONARY

LIVORNESE	Style of Leghorn (Livorno).
Cacciucco:	A fish stew with garlic & peppers. Served with oven baked slices of bread.
Sauce for pasta	Mushrooms, cheese & tomato.
LODI GRANA	Lombardy equivalent of Parmesan cheese.
LOMBARDA	Style of Lombardy.
Tortelli alla:	Pasta cases stuffed with pumpkin, macaroons, mustard, lemon & cheese.
LOMBATA	Literally "loin". Usually Lombata di Coniglio — fillets from back of wild rabbit.
LOMBATINE	Small steaks of beef from rib end of sirloin. French "entrecôte".
LOMBO	Loin.
LONZA	Fillet of pork cured like ham with spices, wine & garlic.
LUCANIA	Olives, anchovies, garlic & oil for pasta.
LUCCHESE	
Lasagnette del:	Pasta with ricotta cheese & chicken livers.
LUCCIO	Pike.
arrostito alla "Luigi Veronelli":	Stuffed with pork & baked. Mushrooms & potatoes.
LUCULLO-IANI	
Banane:	Banana skin filled with baked mashed banana with eggs, apricot sauce & curaçao.
Conchiglie di scampi:	Large shrimps with mushrooms &

ITALIAN

	cheese sauce in scallop shells.
Spiedini:	Chicken livers, smoked tongue & cheese on a skewer. White sauce & crumbs.
LUGANEGA-ICA	Sweet sausages.
LUIGI VERONELLI	A great Italian food & wine expert.
Filetti di tacchino:	Turkey breast oven cooked, wrapped in pancakes & fried in crumbs. Onion sauce.
Funghi alla:	Hot. Mushrooms fried with onions, garlic, tomatoes, vinegar.
Linguine alla:	Pasta with clams, mussels, shrimps, squid, white wine, onion & garlic. Tomatoes, tuna fish, anchovy butter & parsley.
Luccio arrostito alla:	Pike stuffed with pork & baked. Mushrooms & potatoes.
Medaglioni di aragosta alla:	Lobster paste fried in crumbs with lobster slices. On fried bread.
Pernice alla:	Partridge casseroled with sausages, cabbage, pork, carrots, herbs & wine.
Sogliola alla:	Sole egg & crumbed. Mushrooms, shrimps, cream & fried bread.
LUMACHE	Snails.
Or	Pasta shaped like snail shells. Important to know which you are getting!

M

MACCARELLO   Mackerel.

DINERS' DICTIONARY

MACCHERON-CINI	A fairly small tubular pasta — between Bucatini and Maccheroni.
MACCHERONI	A moderate sized tubular pasta.
alla salsa di cognac:	With brandy sauce.
"cu" a seccia:	With cuttlefish.
ai quattro formaggi:	With four cheeses. Specialty of Naples.
MADRILENA Arance alla:	Orange rice pudding.
MAGGIORANA	Sweet marjoram. Origanum marjorana.
MAGRO	Literally "of the thin" or "a fasting dish". Not necessarily for the slimmer! Usually meaning containing no meat.
Cappon:	Fish Salad. Specialty of Genoa. Very variable. Hard biscuit (cookie) or bread base. Potatoes, carrots, artichokes, celery, beet, beans, cauliflower & olives. White fish, lobster, shrimps & crab. Oil, vinegar, parsley, garlic (in quantity), eggs, anchovies, herbs & capers. A very filling garlic dish!
Pomodori di:	Tomatoes stuffed with tuna fish in oil, peppers & anchovy butter.
MAIALE	Pig — Pork.
Arista di maiale cardi:	Roast pork with cardoons.
Arista di maiale alla Toscana:	Roast pork with black-eyed beans.
Carre di:	Loin.
Costoletto-ini di:	Chops.
Fettine di:	Thin cutlets.
Filetto di:	Loin.
Intingolo di:	Cut into pieces.
Involtini di:	Thin slices rolled & stuffed.
Petto di:	Belly.

ITALIAN

Prosciutto di:	The hindquarter. The English "leg", the American "ham". May be cooked fresh — fresco, smoked or as Prosciutto di Parma — lightly salted, not smoked.
Quadrello di:	Loin.
MAIONESE	Mayonnaise.
MALTAGLIATI	A short tubular pasta. Also called PENNE.
MANDORLE	Almonds.
MANICHE	A short fat tubular pasta.
al Ortolana:	With peas & artichokes.
MANTECATO	Salt cod purée. (Venice).
MANZO	Beef. See also BUE.
Arrosta:	Roast beef.
Bistecca di:	Steak — can be of minced beef.
Braciola di:	Thin slices. Often stuffed — FARCITE.
Costata di:	Rib.
Intingolo di:	Cut into pieces.
Lesso:	Boiled,
Lesso alla Napolitana:	Boiled with tomatoes, garlic, oregano & parsley.
Lesso in polpetti alla Romana:	Meatballs fried in crumbs. Cheese & tomatoes.
Lombatines di:	Small steaks from rib end of sirloin. French "entrecôte".'
Ripieno arrosta:	Roast beef stuffed with chicken liver, ham, cheese, egg, bread & vegetables.
Spalla di:	Shoulder.
MARE	Sea.
Fritto Misto di:	Mixed fried fish. Red mullet or goatfish, squid & shrimps.
Frutti di:	French "fruits de mer". Shellfish uni-or bi-valve. Possibly with crustaceans.
MARIA TERESA Coppa:	Cup of peach compôte, Drambuie,

DINERS' DICTIONARY

	peach ice cream & almonds.
Insalata:	Celeriac, lettuce, eggs, chicken, truffles, mayonnaise & vinaigrette.
Filetti di sogliola:	Fillet of sole baked with mushrooms, shallots & wine. Cream & egg sauce.
Costolette di vitello:	Veal chops fried in crumbs. Cheese & tomatoes. Anchovies.
MARINA	
Filetti di sogliola:	Fillet of sole fried. Mussels & shrimps. Truffles & whisky.
MARINATO	Marinaded & served cold.
MARMORA	Striped bream. A seafish.
MARRO	Veal stuffed with ham, garlic & anchovies.
MARSALA	Strong, sweet fortified wine similar to sherry.
MARSIONI	Small sea or river fish.
MASCARPONE	A product of cows milk which is a mixture between cream & cheese. (Lombardy).
MATRICIANA	Corruption of all'Amariciana.
MAZZAFEGATI	Liver sausage.
MAZZANCOLLE (or MAZZACUOGNO)	Large prawns or shrimps.
MAZZARELLA	Lamb offal or variety meats with eggs & spices.
MEDAGLIONI	French "medaillons". Small steaks (usually of veal). Can also refer to lobster flesh.
di vitello alla Bolognese:	Small veal steaks fried in crumbs. With ham, cheese & truffles.
di vitello alla Piemontese:	Small veal steaks fried in crumbs. With cheese, truffles and a cheese risotto.

ITALIAN

di aragosta "Luigi Veronelli":	Lobster paste fried in crumbs with lobster slices. On fried bread.
MELAGRANATA	Pomegranate.
MELANZANE	Aubergine or egg plant. Served in a variety of ways.
Dorati alla Milanese:	Fried in egg & crumbs.
Farciti all'Italiana:	Stuffed with onion, tomato & garlic. Baked.
Farciti alla Siciliana:	Stuffed with onion, tomato, garlic & anchovies. Baked.
Siciliana:	With cheese, eggs, tomatoes & basil. Baked. Tomato sauce.
alla Napoletana:	Oven cooked with tomato, cheese & basil.
MELBA Nocciole d'agnello:	Small fried lamb steaks on fried bread with baked tomatoes stuffed with chicken, mushrooms & truffles. Madeira sauce. Braised lettuce.
Pesche:	Cooked half peaches, raspberry purée, kirsch & vanilla ice cream.
MELE	Apples.
MELONE	Melon.
MERENDA	Luncheon. Midday meal.
MERINGA	Meringue. However MERINGA ITALIANA is a form of icing from egg whites which is not cooked.
MENTA	Mint. Mentha viridis.

DINERS' DICTIONARY

MENTA ROMANA (or MENTUCCIA)	Peppermint. Mentha peperita.
MERLANGO	Hake. A sea fish.
MERLANO	Whiting. A sea fish. Silver hake.
MERLI	Blackbirds.
MERLUZZO	Hake. A sea fish.
MESSICANI	Stuffed veal rolls.
MEZZA ZITA	A tubular pasta larger than Maccheroni.
MEZZEUOVA SODE	Literally "half hard boiled" eggs. Served stuffed & cold. Like FARCIA.
MIELE	Honey.
MIGLIACCIO	A cake of chestnut flour.
MILANESE	Milan style.
Aspergi:	Asparagus with cheese, hazel nut butter & fried eggs.
Cardi:	Cardoons with cheese & hazel nut butter.
Fritto Misto:	Fried veal, sweetbreads, cockscombs & vegetables.
Melanzane Dorati alla:	Aubergines or egg plant fried in egg & crumbs.
Minestre Trippa alla:	Soup of tripe, cabbage, white haricot beans, vegetables, garlic & cheese.
Minestre (Verzata):	Soup of savoy cabbage, sausage, cheese, bacon, herbs. Browned bread.
Minestrone:	Soup of pork, onions, leeks, tomatoes, potatoes, carrots, asparagus, courgettes or zucchini, broad or shell beans, green beans, peas, cheese, celery & rice.
Osso Buco:	Stewed veal bones & marrow with herbs, wine, tomatoes, garlic, parsley & lemon rind.
Risotto:	Rice dish with beef marrow (or

ITALIAN

	chicken), wine, saffron & cheese.
Spinaci alla:	Spinach browned with cheese. Scrambled eggs.
Trippa alla:	Tripe in oil with onion, garlic, parsley, cheese & a lot of meat sauce.
Verzata alla:	Minestre — see above.
Costolette di Vitello:	Veal cutlets in crumbs.
Fegato di Vitello:	Veal liver sliced, marinaded & fried in crumbs.
MILLE RIGHI	Short elbow shaped ribbed pasta.
MINESTRE	Soup. Usually regional specialties.
Casalinga:	Haricot beans, tomatoes & herbs. Pasta.
Broccoli alla Romana:	Broccoli, ham, cheese, garlic. Pasta.
Contadina:	Chick peas, lettuce heart, ham, tomatoes, cheese. Bread.
Ceci Romana:	Chick peas, rosemary, garlic, anchovies. Pasta.
Ceci Toscana:	Chick peas, rosemary, garlic, anchovies, tomatoes. Pasta.
Fave Romana:	Broad or shell beans, pork, tomatoes, cheese. Pasta.
Genovese:	Made from CIMA broth, marjoram, eggs, cheese. Pasta.
Milanese (Verzata):	Savoy cabbage, sausage, cheese, bacon, herbs. Browned bread.
Napolitana:	Chicken, beef, cabbage, chicory, ham, salami, pork, endive.
Romana:	Ham, onion, garlic, tomato, cheese. Pasta.
de Trippa alla Milanese:	Tripe, cabbage, white haricot beans, vegetables, garlic, cheese. Croutons.
Veneta:	1: Red haricot beans, ham, onion, cinnamon. Noodles.
	2: Sausage, turnip, ham, cheese. Rice.

DINERS' DICTIONARY

MINESTRONE	A vegetable soup usually with a starch addition (rice, pasta, beans, potatoes etc.). Always thick.
Genovese:	With pesto (crushed herbs), spinach, beet greens, broad or shell beans, cabbage, potatoes, onions, leeks. Pasta.
Italiana:	Beet greens, pork, onion, ham, haricot beans, courgettes or zucchini. Pasta.
Milanese:	Pork, onion, leeks, tomatoes, potatoes, carrots, asparagus, courgettes or zucchini, broad or shell beans, green beans, peas, cheese, celery. Rice. The Milanese also serve this cold (FREDDO).
Toscana:	Haricot beans, herbs, endive, tomatoes, cheese, onion, parsley, celery. Pasta.
MIRTO	Myrtle. A herb.
MISOLTINI	Salt dried lake sardines (AGONI). Served grilled. (Lake Como).
MITILI	Alternative name for mussels.
MODENESE	Style of Modena.
Costoletti di maiale alla:	Pork chops in wine, rosemary, sage & garlic.
MOLECCHE	Small soft-shelled crabs. Fried. Specialty of Venice.
MONACHINE	Bullfinches.
MONTE BIANCO	A dessert of chestnut purée & whipped cream.
MONTONE	Mutton.
MORBIDELLE	French "quenelles". Small dumplings of forcemeat or fish.
MORENE	Lampreys or Sea-eels.
MORTADELLA	Sausage. Specialty of Bologna. Of pork. May be a mixture of pork, veal, tripe & potatoes.
MOSCARDINI	Small octopus.

alla Genovese:	Cut in strips, stewed in oil with mushrooms, herbs, onion & tomatoes. Croutons.
MOSTARDA DI FRUTTA	Fruit in syrup with garlic & mustard. With cold meat or eels. Specialty of Cremona.
MOUSSE	A smooth rich cream sweet or savory; e.g. liver, chicken, tomato, ham.
MOZZARELLA	Originally a buffalo cheese. White & soft but solid. May leak cream when cut. Eat very fresh.
MUGGINE	Grey mullet. Sea fish.
MUGNAIA	"alla mugnaia" = the French "la meunière". Fish fried in hot oil or butter. Boiling butter poured over it as served.
MULETTE	Salted & smoked pork.
MULETTU	Grey mullet. (Sicily).
MUSCIAMA	Sun-dried dolphin flesh.
MUSCOLI	Alternative name for mussels.
MUSCOLO	Shin of beef.
MUSO	Muzzle of beef.
MUZAO	Grey mullet. (Genoa).

N

NAPOLETANA	Style of Naples.
Baccala alla:	Strips of dried cod cooked in oil. Garlic, tomatoes, black olives, capers & oregano.
Braciola di manzo farcita alla:	Rump steak sliced, rolled & stuffed with nuts, raisins, herbs & garlic.

DINERS' DICTIONARY

Insalata:	Cauliflower head, anchovies, olives, capers & eggs in a salad.
Lasagne alla:	Traditional Naples on Shrove Tuesday. Layers of cheese & ham braised in marsala with pasta.
Costoletti di Maiale alla:	Pork chops in garlic, peppers, tomatoes & mushrooms.
Manzo lesso alla:	Boiled beef with tomatoes, garlic, oregano & parsley.
Melanzane alla:	Oven cooked aubergines or egg plant. Tomato, cheese & basil.
Minestre:	Soup of chicken, beef, cabbage, chicory, ham, salami, pork & endive.
Pasta alla:	With herbs & tomato sauce.
Pizza:	Refer to PIZZA.
Risotto:	Rice dish with wine, cheese, onion, pork, celery, garlic & tomatoes.
Sartu di riso alla:	An open rice pie with rice oven crusted at top. Contains beef, chicken livers, sausage, mushrooms, eggs, onions, tomatoes & cheese.
Stecchi alla:	Aubergines or egg plant, green tomatoes, mozzarella cheese & bread on sticks. Egg & deep fried.
Zeppole alla:	Fried dough rings with sugar.

NASELLO	Whiting or hake.
NEGRETTI	Chocolate almond squares.
NERONE	
Filetti di tacchino alla:	Turkey breasts fried in crumbs & flamed in brandy.

ITALIAN

NEWBOURG	French "Newburg".
Astaco alla:	Cut pieces of lobster fried. Madeira, eggs, cream & paprika.
NINFETTA	Literally "water nymph".
Cozze:	Fried mussels with Worcester sauce.
NINON Albicocche:	Cold sweet. Apricots with almonds, blackcurrant jelly, kirsch & cream.
NIZZARDA	Literally "from Nice". French "Niçoise" but may differ from the French cuisine.
Nocciole d'agnello alla:	Fried small lamb steaks with tomato sauce, nut shaped potatoes browned in butter & green beans.
Bistecche alla:	Fried minced beef with onions & garlic.
Branzinetti alla:	Bass fried with onions, olives, tomatoes & herbs. Anchovy fillets.
Canapes:	Anchovy butter, black olives & chopped onion.
Insalata:	Salad of green beans, potatoes, tomatoes, capers, olives & anchovies.
Ravioli:	Pasta stuffed with beef, beet greens, onions & cheese.
Stoccafisso alla:	Dried cod with garlic, leeks, onions, tomatoes, potatoes, black olives & anchovies.
NOCCIOLE	Hazel nuts. ALSO means small steaks of veal, lamb or pork. French "noisettes".
d'agnello alla Cacciatoro:	Small lamb steaks with onion, white wine, mushrooms, stock & tomato sauce.
d'agnello all'Italiana:	Fried small lamb steaks with fried bread, fried ham & white wine sauce.

DINERS' DICTIONARY

d'agnello Melba:	Small fried lamb steaks on fried bread with baked tomatoes stuffed with chicken, mushrooms & truffles. Madeira sauce. Braised lettuce.
d'agnello Nizzarda:	Fried small lamb steaks with tomato sauce, nut-shaped potatoes browned in butter & green beans.
NOCCIOLINI	Meatballs.
NOCE	Walnut.
NOCE MOSCATA	Nutmeg.
NOCE DI VITELLO	Rolled rump of veal.
NODINI	Veal chops.
NONNA	Literally "grandmother".
Bistecche della:	Minced beef, white sauce, cheese & breadcrumbs.
NOVARRA	A Lombardy town west of Milan.
Biscotti di:	Egg & vanilla biscuit or cookie.

OCA	Goose.
Farcita alla Borghese:	Roast stuffed goose. Stuffing of onions, apples, chestnuts, pine nuts, allspice, pork, goose liver & brandy.
Farcita alla Paesana:	Roast goose stuffed with goose liver, chicken liver, pork, parsley & sage.
OLIO	Oil.
OLIVE	Olive.
Farcite:	Stuffed.
Nere:	Black.
Verde:	Green.

ITALIAN

OLIVETTE	Rolled veal stuffed with capers & anchovies.
OMBRINA	Mediterranean sea fish similar to bass with firm white flesh.
ORATA	Sea bream. Chrysophrys aurata. Similar to Porgy in U.S.A.
alla Casalinga:	Baked with herbs, white wine & anchovy fillets.
alla Contadina:	Casseroled with herbs, wine, onion & tomatoes.
alla Fantasia:	Baked in foil with anchovies.
all'Italiana:	Sliced. In vermouth, mushrooms & cream.
ORECCHIE DI MAIALE	Pig's ear. Usually with lentils or cold with vinaigrette.
ORECCHIETTE	A short tubular pasta.
ai broccoli:	With flowering broccoli. (Sicily).
ORIGANO	Oregano (wild marjoram). Origanum vulgare. Characteristic flavor of Pizza Napoletana.
ORONGE	Edible fungus. Amanita caesarea.
OROLO	Edible fungus.
ORTAGGI Antipasto di:	Truffles, mushrooms, artichokes, fennel, peppers, celery, pickles & dressing.
ORTOLANA Maniche all':	Pasta with peas & artichokes.
ORTOLANI	Small birds.

DINERS' DICTIONARY

OSSO BUCO MILANESE	Specialty of Milan. Often referred to as just OSSO BUCO. A dish of veal bones containing the marrow with herbs, wine, tomatoes, garlic, parsley & lemon rind.
OSTRICA	Mushroom sauce for pasta.
OSTRICHE	Oysters.
OVARINE	Unlaid eggs inside a hen which are somtimes added to RAGU (Bolognese sauce).

P

PADELLA	Frying pan.
PAESANA	Style of the peasant.
Cappone in casseruola alla:	Capon casseroled with wine, tomatoes, ham, courgettes or zucchini & peppers.
Carciofi in spicchi alla:	Artichokes casseroled with pork, onions, potatoes & lettuce.
Carre di Maiale alla:	Roast pork boned. Garlic, thyme, rosemary, bay leaf, stock, white wine.
Pasta alla:	With mushrooms, bacon, tomato, cheese & herb sauce.
Risotto:	Rice dish with asparagus, courgettes or zucchini, broad or shell beans, tomatoes & cheese.
Costoletti di Vitello:	Veal chops casseroled with carrots, leeks, onions, celery & potatoes.
PAGELLO	A sea fish. Spanish bream.

ITALIAN

PAGLIATO	Intestines.
PAGLIETTE	Literally "straw".
al parmigiano:	Cheese straws.
PAILLARD	A veal steak very thin & grilled.
PALAMITA	A sea fish. Bonito. Between mackerel & tuna in size.
PALERMITANA	Style of Palermo (Sicily).
Sarde ripiene alla:	Sardines stuffed with raisins, pine nuts, parsley & anchovies & fried in crumbs.
PALLOTTOLNE	Cheese flavored dumplings.
PALOMBACCI	Wood pigeon. French "palombe".
PALOMBO	Large dogfish or Smooth hound.
PANCETTA	Specialty of Parma made from stomach of pig.
PANDORATO	Bread, cheese & eggs fried with anchovy fillets.
PANE	Bread,
PANE GRATTUGIATO	Breadcrumbs.
PANETTI	Meatballs.
PANETTONE	Flaky pastry loaf with sultanas. Traditional Milan at Christmas.
PANFORTE	A rich sweet. Specialty of Siena.
PANINI	Rolls.
PANINI IMBOTTITO	Sandwiches.
PANNA	Cream.
Acida:	Sour cream.
Fresca:	Fresh.
Montana:	Whipped.
PANERONE	A white version of Gorgonzola cheese.
PANZAROTTI	A Neopolitan dish. Dough with ham & cheese fried in oil.
PAPALINA	Sprat.
PAPARELLE	Legume soup.
PAPAROT	Spinach soup with polenta. Specialty of Venetia Giulia.
PAPPARDELLE	A ribbon-like pasta a little smaller than lasagne.

DINERS' DICTIONARY

PARIGINA	Literally "Parisian".
Costolettine d'agnello alla:	Lamb chops fried in crumbs, with mushrooms & asparagus.
Cozze alla:	Mussels boiled in wine, shallots & thyme.
PARMESAN	The most famous Italian cheese. When cooked it does not form strings. Matured for two years or more. Firm, yellow with tiny holes. Quite unlike the rubbish sold in Britain under this name!
PARMIGIANA	With grated parmesan cheese.
Or	A pie of aubergines or egg plant, cheese, tomato sauce & oil.
PASQUALE	Literally "Easter".
Cosciotto d'agnello:	Braised leg of lamb with marinaded ham inserted into slits. Cooked in white wine.
PASSATELLI	A material similar to pasta made of breadcrumbs, bone marrow, cheese & eggs. Cut like spaghetti. In soup. Specialty of Modena-Bologna area.
Brodo con passatelli alla Marchigiana:	Bouillon with passatelli.
PASTA-E	Literally "dough" and includes the pastry for cakes etc. Usually covers spaghetti etc. — see below.
all'Ouvo:	Egg based pastas made at home.
Asciutta:	Forms a dish in itself.
in Brodo:	Small shaped units in soups.
Ripiena:	Stuffed.
Secca:	Purchased dried pastas. The pasta may be cylindrical-solid like SPAGHETTI. tubular like MACCHERONI. ribbon-like as LASAGNE.

ITALIAN

	short cylinders like MALTAGLIATI.
	cases for stuffing like RAVIOLI.
PASTELLA	Frying batter.
PASTICCIO	Pie.
di Fegatini di pollo:	Chicken liver pie.
di maiale all'Inglese:	Hot pork pie.
PASTINE	Tiny pastas for soups.
PASTO	Food. Meal.
PASTORELLA	Cheese similar to Bel Paese.
PATANE	Sweet potatoes.
PATATE	Potatoes. Almost all methods of cooking are international with conventional French names.
PATE	Correctly refers to concentrated meat or fish oven cooked in a pastry case & served either hot or cold. Loosely used to include meats not in pastry which are served cold — really terrines. Duck, hare, veal, woodcock, onion, shrimp & tongue.
PAVESE-INI	Style of Pavia near Milan.
Biscotti tipo:	Egg, vanilla & almond biscuits or cookies.
Zuppa:	Consomme (chicken or meat or vegetable), with poached egg, grated cheese & fried bread.
PECORINO	Hard sheeps cheese. Used in many Roman specialties.

DINERS' DICTIONARY

PENNE	A short small tubular pasta.
all'Arrabbiatra:	With tomatoes, bacon, garlic, onion & chillies.
PEOCI	Mussels. Venetian name.
PEPE	Pepper.
PEPERONATA	Sweet pepper & tomato stew. (Lombardy).
PEPERONCINO	Chillies.
PEPERONI	Peppers (capsicums).
Gialli:	Yellow peppers.
alla Romana:	Fried in oil with onions & tomatoes.
PERE	Pears.
PERNICE	Partidge.
alla Luigi Veronelli:	Casseroled with sausages, cabbage, pork, carrots, herbs & wine.
PERUGINA	Style of Perugia.
Arista:	Pork roasted in water with fennel & garlic.
Scaloppine alla:	Veal scallops with chicken liver croutons.
PESCANOCE	Nectarine.
PESCATRICE	Angler fish. French "baudroie".
PESCE	Fish.
d'acqua dolce:	Freshwater fish.
di mare:	Sea fish.
Prete:	Weaver fish.
Persico:	Perch. A freshwater fish.
San Pietro:	John Dory. An ugly but tasty sea fish.
alla Casalinga:	Fish mashed with potatoes, eggs & butter. Baked. Fried bread.
PESCHE	Peaches.
Conde:	A hot sweet with creamed rice.
Melba:	Cooked half peaches, raspberries, kirsch & vanilla ice cream.
Rex:	Half peaches cooked in syrup, ice cream, zabaglione, Aurum liqueur, almonds, chocolate & cream.

ITALIAN

Ripiene alla Genovese:	Stuffed with peach, brandy & macaroons. Baked & served warm. Vanilla wafers.
PESTO ALLA GENOVESE	For pastas, soups, fish etc. A blend of basil, spinach, parsley, marjoram, pine nuts, garlic, parmesan & pecorino cheeses, oil & butter.
PETTI DI POLLO	Chicken breasts.
PETTINE	A bi-valve shellfish. Pilgrim scallop.
PETTO	Breast (of lamb, mutton, veal) or belly (of pork).
di vitello ripieno alla Casalinga:	Boned breast of veal stuffed with pork, ham, sausage, garlic & parsley.
PIATTI	Dish.
Farsi:	Dishes to order.
Giorni:	Dishes of the day.
Pronti:	Dishes which are ready.
PICCANTE—I	Piquant. Often with Worcester sauce.
Costolette di maiale alla:	Pork chops with onion, garlic, wine, dill pickles & Worcester sauce.
PICCATA	Small slices of veal cut thinly.
PICCIONCELI	Squabs. Very young pigeons.
alla Buongustaia:	Spatchcocked (split in half) & fried. Brandy, chicken & meat stock, parsley.
PICCIONI	Adult pigeons.
Selvatico:	Wild or wood pigeons.
con piselli:	Casseroled with tongue, ham, onions, white wine, peas & basil.
PIEDINI DI MAIALE	Pigs trotters or feet.
PIEMONTESE	Style of Piedmont.
Bagna Cauda:	A hot dip of garlic, anchovies, & truffles for cardoons or celery. Traditional on Christmas Eve.

DINERS' DICTIONARY

Fasoeil al Furn:	Red haricot beans cooked very slowly with pork rind or bacon, parsley, garlic, pepper, cinnamon, cloves & mace.
Fonduta:	Cheese, milk & egg melted on toast.
Fritto:	A simple pasta-like mixture fried.
Lasagne:	Meat sauce, truffles & cheese with pasta.
Ravioli:	Pasta stuffed with rice, beef, cabbage, vegetables & cheese.
Risotto:	Simple rice dish with lobster & truffles.
Filetti di Tacchino alla:	Turkey breasts fried in crumbs with cheese & truffles.
Medaglioni di Vitello alla:	Small veal steaks fried in crumbs with cheese & truffles. With a cheese risotto.
PIGNATELLI	Pastry mixed with cheese & ham. Fried in deep fat as tiny dumplings.
PIGNOLI	Pine nuts.
PILAFF	Rice. Boiled, washed & then oven cooked in stock & butter.
PINCISGRASSI	Pasta cooked in the oven with meat gravy & cream sauce. (Abruzzi).
PINOCCATE	Pine nut & almond paste biscuits or cookies.
PINOLI	Pine nuts.
PIOPPINO	Aegerita. A wild or cultivated edible fungus. Agrocybe aegerita.
PISELLI	Peas.
PISTOU	Soup of fried beans, potatoes & tomatoes. With vermicelli & paste of garlic, basil & tomatoes. (Genoa).

ITALIAN

PIZZA—E—ETTE	Literally "pie". In its basic form, bread dough spread with tomatoes & mozzarella cheese baked in a hot oven. Very variable. Naples is the home of Pizza. In Rome, it may be made with onions & oil only. In Liguria, with onions, black olives & anchovies. Pizzette is a small pizza.
alla Napoletana:	With tomatoes, garlic & oregano.
alla Napoletana Marinara:	As the above plus anchovies.
alla Napoletana Fantasia:	Mashed potato in the dough. With tomatoes, basil, garlic, parmesan & anchovies.
PIZZAIOLA	
Baccala alla:	Baked dried cod with tomatoes & mixed herbs on top.
Bistecche alla:	Steak spread with tomato, garlic & oregano. (Naples).
Costata di bue alla:	Sliced beef with pizzaiola sauce.
Salsa:	Sauce of oil, tomatoes, chopped garlic, basil, parsley, oregano & pepper.
PIZZELLE	Small pizza dough packed with filling.
Casalinghe Napolitane:	With endive, garlic, anchovies, capers, olives & raisins.
POLENTA	A boiled product of maize flour used as a bread substitue.
Ciociara:	Polenta in the oven with minced beef, tomato sauce, mushrooms, sausage & cheese.
con gli uccelli:	Lombardy specialty. Fried with onion & mushrooms. Small song birds on top.
Pasticciata:	Layers of polenta, white sauce & mushrooms, baked in oven with cheese on top. Specialty of Milan.
POLIPORO	Highly colored edible fungus.

DINERS' DICTIONARY

POLLAME	Poultry.
POLLASTRA	Pullets. Young hens 8 months old.
POLLO	Chicken. Several hundred methods of preparation, many of international cuisine with French names.
Costolette di:	Breast and wing.
Filetti di:	Breast.
Petti di:	Breast.
Saute:	Fried in oil or butter.
Spezzatini di:	Fried, breast removed & served.
allo Spiedo:	On a spit.
Pollastra:	pullets.
Cappone:	capons.
POLMONE	Lungs.
POLPETTE	Fried meat ball. Usually veal. French "fricadelle".
POLPETTINE	Dumpling. Can be of vegetable e.g. Polpettine di spinaci.
POLPETTONE	Meat loaf with breadcrumbs.
Or	Sausage of mixed fish.
di tonno:	Of tuna fish.
POLPI—O	Octopus.
di scoglio:	Rock octopus.
POMODORI—O	Tomatoes.
all'Italiana:	Cold. Under-ripe plum tomatoes, garlic, oil & basil.
alla Siciliana:	Baked with a stuffing of onion, anchovies, parsley, capers & olives.
di Magro:	Stuffed with tuna fish & peppers.
con riso alla Romana:	Stuffed with rice, garlic, basil & tomato sauce.
POMPELMO	Grapefruit.
PORCEDDU	Sardinian roast suckling pig.
PORCELLINO	Suckling pig. Under 8 weeks old.
Cosciotto di:	Haunch of suckling pig.
PORCHETTA	Roast suckling pig.
PORCINI	A red capped mushroom. Boletus edulis.

PORRI	Leeks.
PRANZO	Dinner.
PRATAIOLO	Field mushroom. Agaricus campestris.
PREZZEMOLO	Parsley.
PRIMA COLAZIONI	Breakfast.
PRIMAVERILE (or PRIMIZIE)	Literally "first fruits".
Controfiletto di bue:	Sirloin steak with ham & salt pork marinaded & oven cooked. Green beans & potatoes.
Costata di bue con:	Roasted rib of beef. Carrots, green beans, artichokes & peas.
PROSCIUTTO	The hindquarter of pig. The English "leg", the American "ham". May be cooked fresh — fresco, smoked or as Prosciutto di Parma, lightly salted — not smoked.
di Cinghiale:	Smoked wild boar ham. Specialty of Sardinia.
PROVATURE	Buffalo cheese. Must be fresh.
PROVENZALE	Style of Provence. French "Provençale" but may differ from French cuisine.
Anguilla alla:	Eels fried with parsley, onion & garlic. Breadcrumbs. The classic French dish has tomatoes which the Italian may not contain.
Cozze:	Mussels oven roasted with minced snails. Crumbs.
Salsa:	Sauce for eggs or boiled meat. Vinegar, oil, pepper, tomatoes, egg, capers, parsley & garlic.
PROVOLA	Buffalo cheese. Eaten fresh.
PROVOLONE	Buffalo cheese. Eaten fresh.
PRUGNE	Prunes.

DINERS' DICTIONARY

PUDDINGHINOS A PINU	Baked stuffed young chicken. (Sardinia).
PULCINO	Spring chicken.
PUNTA	Cold roasted CIMA.
PUNTI	Literally "tip". Used in reference to asparagus. Punti di asparagi — asparagus tips.
PUREA	Purée,
PURGATORIO	With a very spicy sauce.

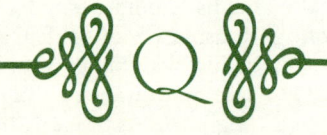

Q

QUADRELLO	Loin & best end of lamb or mutton or loin of pork. Also called COSTOLETTE.
QUAGLIA	Quail. Many recipes which are self-descriptive e.g. Quaglia in casseruola — casseroled quail.
QUAGLIETTE	Literally "little quails". Small pieces of lamb, pork, or veal on skewers.
QUARESIMALE Antipasto:	Literally "of Lent". Cold carp, eggs, mushrooms, artichokes, olives, boiled eggs, mayonnaise.
QUARTO d'agnello arrosta al prezzemolo:	Literally "quarter". Leg (of lamb). Roast leg of lamb with parsley.

ITALIC

R

RADICCHIE	Radishes.
RAFANO	Radishes or Horseradish.
RAGGIO DI SOLE	Literally "rays of the sun".
Baccala al:	Dried cod oven baked with onions, garlic, capers, pine nuts, raisins & anchovy paste.
RAGU	Stew. Also proper name of Bolognese sauce.
d'agnello a bianco:	Lamb stew. Onions, herbs, potatoes, parsley, & white stock.
d'agnello buona donna:	Lamb stew. Potatoes, garlic, herbs, onions & brown stock.
di bue alla Borghese:	Rump steak cut up & stewed with vegetables & herbs.
d'oca:	Goose stew with chestnuts or vegetables.
RAMOLACCIO	
RANE	Horseradish.
Cosce de:	Frogs.
Costolettine:	Frogs legs.
RAPE	Turnips.
RAVANELLI	Radishes.
RAVIGGIOLA	Tuscany sheeps cheese.
RAVIOLI	Square pasta cases with fillings. Similar to Agnolotti but should contain the soft sheep's cheese ricotta & possibly spinach.
Genovese:	Stuffed with beet greens, spinach, chicken, sausage & cheese.

Nizzarda:	Stuffed with beef, beet greens, onions & cheese.
Piemontese:	Stuffed with rice, beef, cabbage, vegetables & cheese.
RAVIOLINI	Tiny ravioli used as a soup garnish.
RAZZA	Skate.
REALE	Small compounds of meat or vegetables used as soup garnish.
Albicocche alla:	Cold apricots. Kirsch, aniseed liqueur, raspberries, sponge cake & nuts.
REGINA	Large carp. (Perugia).
REINA	Sea fish.
REX	
Pesche:	Half peaches cooked in syrup. Ice cream, zabaglione, Aurum liqueur, almonds, chocolate & cream.
RICCA	Literally "like the wealthy". With a side dish of braised celery as in Agnello brodettata alla ricca.
Bue brasato al:	Beef braised in wine, brandy & herbs. Mushrooms & onions.
RICCI	Sea urchins. Coral (eggs or roe) eaten raw. Delicious!
RICCIARELLI	Almond biscuits or cookies.
RICOTTA	Soft sheep's cheese.
RIGAGLIE	Giblets, liver, heart & lungs of a bird.
RIGATONI	The largest of the short tubular pastas.
RISI—O	Rice. Name of a number of non-risotto dishes.
al Salto:	Fried rice. (Lombardy).
Pilaff:	Pilaff rice.
e Bisi:	Rice & green peas. Similar to a risotto — soup eaten with a fork! (Venice).
Bomba di:	Oven cooked pigeons with rice. Specialty of Parma.
Sartu di riso alla Napoletana:	An open rice pie with the rice oven crusted at the top. Contains beef,

ITALIAN

	chicken livers, sausage, mushrooms, eggs, onions, tomatoes & cheese. Specialty of Naples.
RISOTTO	A dish of rice served alone which has absorbed the concentrate of some product. The simplest is with butter, white wine & saffron. It is to the north what pasta is to the south.
in Capro Roman:	With mutton, tomatoes, wine & cheese. (Venice).
alla Genovese:	With meat sauce, onion, sausage meat, wine, peas, artichokes, mushrooms & cheese.
alla Milanese:	With beef marrow (or chicken), wine, saffron & cheese.
alla Napoletana:	With wine, cheese, onion, pork, celery, garlic & tomatoes.
alla Paesana:	With asparagus, courgettes or zucchini, broad or shell beans, tomatoes & cheese.
alla Piemontese:	Simple with lobster & truffles.
di Secole:	With scraps of beef or veal, wine, celery, carrot. (Venice).
alla Siciliana:	With broad or shell beans, artichokes, onion & cheese.
con peoci alla Veneta:	With fish stock, mussels & garlic.
Verde:	With spinach, celery, carrot, onion & meat sauce.
alla Veronese:	Simple with ham & mushroom sauce.
RISTRETTO	Consommé. Clear soup.
ROBIOLA	A soft runny cheese with a red casing. (Lombardy & Piedmont). Edible fresh or old.
ROGNONE	Kidneys. Usually calves'kidneys.
ROMANA	Style of Rome.
Agnello alla:	Leg of lamb in cubes baked in spiced crumbs.

DINERS' DICTIONARY

Barchette alla:	Chicken, truffle & mushroom tartlets. Marsala sauce & parmesan cheese.
Bocconotti di ricotta alla:	Cold cheese & fruit tart.
Broccoli	Broccoli cooked in wine & garlic.
Brodetto alla:	Beef, lamb & herb soup. Traditional at Easter.
Fritto alla:	Fried chicken, tongue & cheese sauce.
Fritto Misto alla:	Fried brains, sweetbreads, kidneys & vegetables.
Manzo lesso in polpette alla:	Beef meatballs fried in crumbs. Cheese & tomatoes.
Minestre Broccoli alla:	Soup of broccoli, ham, cheese, garlic & pasta.
Minestre Ceci alla:	Soup of chick peas, rosemary, garlic, anchovies & pasta.
Minestre:	Soup of ham, onions, garlic, tomatoes, cheese & pasta.
Pasta alla:	With mushroom, meat & chicken sauce.
Peperoni alla:	Peppers fried in oil with onions & tomatoes.
Pomodori con riso alla:	Tomatoes stuffed with rice, garlic, basil & tomato sauce.
Saltimbocca alla:	Thin slices of veal folded in half, stuffed with ham, sage & white wine & fixed with a toothpick.
Sarde ripiene alla:	Sardines stuffed with spinach & cream. Fried in crumbs.

Spinaci alla:	Spinach with garlic, ham, pine nuts & raisins.
Trippa alla moda:	Tripe in oil & butter, onions, garlic, parsley, cheese, chicken stock. Chopped mint.
ROMBETTO	Small turbot or slice of turbot.
ROMBO	Turbot. Large saltwater flat fish.
Fricassea di rombetto del Buongustaio:	Sliced. In butter with sole, mussels, onions, mushrooms & cream. (Does such a good fish need all this?).
farcito all'Italiana:	Filleted, stuffed & baked. Lobster sauce.
ROMBO LISCIO	Brill.
ROSETTO	A small transparent fish. A Goby.
ROSPO	Venetian name of Angler fish (PESCATRICE).
RUCHETTA (or RUCOLA) (or RUGHETTA)	Rocket. Eruca sativa. A herb, the leaves of which are used in salad.
RUTA	Rue. A bitter herb. Often added to GRAPPA.

SALAME—I	A sausage produced by pork butchers. Usually served cold as part of antipasta.
di Fabriano:	Pork and youngish beef. (Ancona. Marche).
di Felino:	An irregular shape. Lean pork, white wine & little garlic.

DINERS' DICTIONARY

di Genovese:	Pork, beef & fat.
di Milano:	Pork, beef, fat, pepper, garlic & wine.
di Napolitana:	As the above but more pepper.
di Sardo:	Sardinian. Pork with red pepper.
di Ungherese:	Hungarian. Meat chopped very finely with paprika pepper, garlic & white wine.
SALATO	Salt or salted.
SALCRAUTO	Sauerkraut. Fermented cabbage with juniper berries & pepper.
SALE	Salt. (Purchased, would you believe, at the Tobacconists! — State monopoly).
SALMONE	Salmon.
SALSA	Sauces. Most are international. Only Italian specialties and variations are named below:
di Bastarda:	Milk, flour, butter, egg yolks & lemon juice.
di Bolognese:	Ham, onion, celery, carrot, garlic, beef, mushrooms, wine, parsley, marjoram, nutmeg, tomatoes. Called RAGU.
di Diavola:	For chicken etc. Wine, vinegar, onion, thyme, bay leaf, pepper, cayenne, tabasco & parsley.
di Fantasia:	For cold fish. Oil, egg yolk, mustard, lemon juice, basil, shallots, egg whites, Worcester sauce.
di Genovese:	For cold fish. Pistachio nuts, pine nuts, white sauce, egg yolks, lemon, herb purée.
di Mornay:	Simple white sauce with cream, butter & parmesan cheese.
di Pizzaiola:	Oil, tomatoes, chopped garlic, basil, parsley, oregano & pepper.
di Provenzale:	For eggs or boiled meat. Vinegar, oil, pepper, tomatoes, eggs, capers, parsley & garlic.

ITALIAN

SALSICCIA — E	Highly spiced sausage.
Bucatini con:	Pasta with sausage & tomatoes.
con fagioli stufati in umido:	Pork sausage & beans.
SALSINA	Extract or paste.
di Pomodoro:	Tomato paste or concentrate.
SALTIMBOCCA	Thin slices of veal folded in half, stuffed & fixed with a toothpick (new — one trusts!).
alla Romana:	Stuffed with ham, sage & white wine.
SALVIA	Sage.
SAMBUCO	Elderberry.
SANATO	Very young calf meat.
SANGUIN	Edible fungus. Orange milk cap. Lactarius deliciosa.
SANGUINACCIO	Black pudding or blood sausage.
SANTOREGGIA	Savory. A herb.
SARDĀ-E	Sardines.
SARDINA	Sardines.
alla Contadina:	Fried with tomatoes, garlic, parsley & basil.
Genovese:	Stuffed with cheese, parsley, basil, oregano, & fried in crumbs.
ripiene alla Palermitana:	Stuffed with raisins, pine nuts, parsley & anchovy. Fried in crumbs.
ripiene alla Romana:	Stuffed with spinach in cream. Fried in crumbs.
SARDENARA	Ligurian form of Pizza.

DINERS' DICTIONARY

SARTU di riso alla Napolitana:	A specialty of Naples. An open rice pie with the rice oven crusted at the top. Contains beef, chicken livers, sausage, mushrooms, eggs, onions, tomatoes & cheese.
SATICULANO	Other name of Naples cheese — Caso Forte.
SAUTE	Same as French "sauté". Small pieces of one kind of meat or vegetable tossed in a frying pan of butter, oil or fat.
SAVARIN	Cake from a yeast dough which is round & deep. May be soaked in liqueur and/or with fruit & cream.
SAVOIARDA	Style of Savoy. Also Lady Fingers biscuits or cookies.
Fritatta:	Omelette with pork, potatoes, leeks, parsley & cheese.
SCALOGNA	Shallots.
SCALOPPE	Slices of veal from inside cut of the leg. Escalope.
Milanese:	Fried in egg & crumbs.
SCALOPPINE	Small thin slices. Same as PICCATE.
di animella di vitello:	Of sweetbreads.
di lepre:	Of hare.
di vitello:	Of veal.
SCAMORZA	South Italian cow cheese.
SCAMPI	Medium sized (6 inches long) crustaceans found only in the Adriatic. Similar (but not in taste) to Dublin Bay prawns & French "langoustine".
Spiedini di scampi "Villa Sassi":	Tails grilled on skewers with garlic, brandy, Worcester sauce, anchovy butter, mustard & lemon juice.
SCAPECE	Fish pickled with saffron.
SCAR(I)OLA	Curly lettuce.

ITALIAN

SCIROPPO	Syrup of sugar, water & egg for sweetening.
SCIULE PIENE	Onions stuffed with macaroons, cheese, sultanas & egg. Specialty of Piedmont.
SCORFANO	Rascasse of France. Scorpion Fish.
SCORZETTE	Candied peel.
SCORZONERA	Similar to the oyster plant or vegetable oyster. Long rooted vegetable of delicate flavor.
Bigne di:	Salsify fritters.
SCOTTADITO	Literally "burnt".
Costolettine d'agnello a:	Lamb chops grilled till just black on outside & tender pink inside.
SEDANI	Celery.
SELLA	Saddle of lamb or mutton.
SELVAGGINA	Venison. Deer meat (can mean other game).
SEMOLINA	Small grains of wheat left after sifting flour. Used for gnocchi, cous-cous & other foods.
SEMPLICE	Literally "pure".
Aringhe alla:	Salt herrings alone.
SENAPE	Mustard.
SEPPIA-E	Cuttlefish. Similar to squid.
SEPPIOLINE	Baby cuttlefish. (CALAMARI).
SERPENTARIA	Tarragon. Artemisia dracunculus.
SFOGLIATELLE	A Neopolitan dish. Pastry filled with sweetened cheese & candied fruit.
SFORMATO DI VITELLO	Sliced veal & courgettes or zucchini. Baked with cheese.
SFORMATI	A cross between a soufflé and a pudding. Vegetables, chicken, bird liver, cheese. Peas a popular one.
SGOMBRO	Mackerel.
SICCIA	Cuttlefish.
SICILIANA	From Sicily.

DINERS' DICTIONARY

Broccoli alla:	Broccoli casseroled with onions, olives, anchovies & Caciocavallo cheese.
Cannoli alla:	A pastry filled with ricotta cheese, fruit & nuts. Fried in deep fat.
Melanzane farciti alla:	Aubergines or egg plant stuffed with onions, tomatoes, garlic & anchovies.
Pasta alla:	With tomatoes, courgettes or zucchini, olives, peppers, capers, garlic, basil & anchovies.
Pomodori alla:	Baked tomatoes stuffed with onion, anchovies, parsley, capers & olives.
Stoccafisso alla:	Dried cod with onions, garlic, wine, tomatoes, potatoes, black olives, capers, pine nuts & raisins.
SIERO DEL LATTE	Buttermilk.
SOFFIONCINI	Similar to dumplings.
SOFFIONE	Dandelion.
SOFFRITTO	Onion sauce.
SOGLIOLA	Sole. Large selection of international dishes. See also FILETTI DI SOGLIOLA.
alla "Luigi Veronelli":	In egg & crumbs with mushrooms, shrimps, cream & fried bread.
SOIA	Soy. Soya bean.
SOPPRESSE-ATA	Pork & beef salami — highly flavored. (Verona, Padua & Veneto).
SOSPIRI	Literally "sighs". Savory custard on toast.
SOTT'ACETI	Vegetable pickles.
SOTTO LA CAMPANA	
Filetti di pollo:	Fried breast of chicken with mushrooms & cream. Served under small glass bowls.
SPADA	Swordfish. Mostly found in Sicily and

ITALIAN

	very good.
SPAGHETTI	Probably the best known pasta. Between bucatini & vermicelli in size.
con aglio, olio e peperoncino:	With garlic, oil & chillies.
al'Amatriciana:	With bacon & tomatoes.
con cacio e pepe:	With cheese & black pepper. (Latium).
alla Carbonara:	With bacon, eggs and butter or cream.
alla Cavalleggera:	With eggs & walnuts.
con olio e aglio:	With oil & garlic.
con salsa alla Bolognese:	With bolognese sauce.
SPALLA	Shoulder.
SPANNOCCHIO	Very large shrimps.
SPEZIE	Spices in general.
SPEZZATO	Chopped small.
SPIEDINI-O	Deep fried. On a spit or skewer. French "en brochette".
Beccaccina allo:	Snipe on a spit. Entrails on toast.
Luculliana:	Chicken liver, smoked tongue, cheese. White sauce, crumbs.
di scampi "Villa Sassi":	Large shrimps tails on skewers grilled. With garlic, brandy, Worcester sauce, anchovy butter, mustard & lemon juice.
SPIGOLA	Sea bass. French "loup". Also BRANZINO.
SPINACI	Spinach.
alla Milanese:	With cheese browned with scrambled eggs.
alla Romana:	With garlic, ham, pine nuts & raisins.
SPUGNOLA ROTUNDA	Morel. Edible fungus. Morchella deliciosa.
SPUMA	Mousse.
SPUMONE-I	Ice cream filled with cream, brandied fruit or nuts & other flavored ice creams.

DINERS' DICTIONARY

SQUADRO	Monk fish.
STARNA	Partridge.
STECCHI-INI	Literally "sticks". Similar to Spiedi. Wooden skewers with savory items deep fried.
alla Bolognese:	Veal, sausage, gruyère & bread on sticks. Egg & crumbs & fried.
alla Genovese:	Chicken livers, sweetbreads, tongue & gruyère on sticks. Cheese sauce & crumbs. Deep fried.
alla Napoletana:	Aubergines or egg plant, green tomatoes, mozzarella cheese & bread on sticks. Egged & deep fried.
STOCCAFISSO	Stockfish. Dried cod which has not been salted (unlike BACCALA).
alla Nizzarda:	With garlic, leeks, onions, tomatoes, potatoes, black olives & anchovies.
alla Siciliana:	Onions, garlic, wine, tomatoes, potatoes, black olives, capers, pine nuts & raisins.
STORIONE	Sturgeon.
STRACCHINO	Cheese from warm cows milk. From Lombardy (Taleggio).
STRACCIATA	Strips of lettuce or savory (herb) cooked in butter. Soup garnish.
STRACCIATELLA	A soup with eggs, semolina, cheese & nutmeg added to broth to form a fairly solid entity.
STRACOTTO	Beef stew.
STUFATO–INO	Stewed or braised.
SUCCO	Juice e.g. succo di pomodoro — tomato juice.
SUCCUTUNDU	Balls of semolina in concentrated stock. Specialty of Sardinia.
SUGO	Stock or sauce.
di carne:	Gravy.
SUPPLI	Ball of rice, ham, cheese or other savory & deep fried. Specialty of Rome.

ITALIAN

SUSINE	Plums.
SUSINE VERDI	Greengages.

T

TACCHINO	Turkey. See under ALETTE & FILETTI.
Alette di:	Wing.
Filetti di:	Breast.
TACCULA	Roast small blackbirds & thrushes in containers of myrtle leaves. Specialty of Sardinia.
TAGLIARINI	The smallest of the ribbon pastas.
freddi estivi:	Cold summer pasta. With garlic, parsley, basil, oil & tomato sauce. Served cool.
TAGLIATELLE	Ribbon pasta larger than Tagliarini.
TANUTA	Black bream.
TARTARA	Tartare sauce.
Bistecche alla:	Raw fillet of beef. Tartare sauce. Brandy. Worcester sauce.
TARTELETTE	Tartlets. Small tarts.
all'Italiana:	Tomato sauce, wine, ham, tongue, mushrooms & cheese as filling.
TARTUFI	Truffles.
TARTUFOLI	Small clam. Genoa name. Venus verrucosa.
TAZZA	In a cup.
TEGAME—INO	Two-handled egg frying dish.
TEGLIA	Pie dish.
Acciughe in:	Anchovies baked in oil, garlic & breadcrumbs.
TELLINE	Wedge shell. Similar to mussel.
TEMOLI	Grayling. Freshwater fish.

DINERS' DICTIONARY

TENERONI	End of rib with breast meat. Riblets. Usually veal — Teneroni di vitello.
TERRINA	A paté with no pastry. Concentrate of pounded meat of liver, rabbit, hare, pork etc.
TESTA	Head.
THERMIDOR Astaco alla:	Lobster oven cooked. With mustard & cheese sauce.
TIMBALLI—O	Thick crusted pie served hot. Filled with pasta, meat, game, fish, vegetables, poultry etc. Sartu of Naples is an unusual timballo.
TIMO	Thyme.
TINCA	Tench. Freshwater fish.
TOMINI	Goats cheese with pepper. (Piedmont).
TONNARELLE	A thin cut pasta served with sauce.
TONNELLINI	Pasta. Match-like noodles served with a sauce.
TONNETTO	A seafish. Similar to mackerel. May be small tuna.
TONNO	Tunny fish or tuna.
TOPINAMBURI	Jerusalem artichokes.
TORDI	Thrushes.
TORDI MATTI	Veal on skewers.
TORRESANI	Pigeons.
TORRONE	Nougat.
TORTA PASQUALINA	Easter cake. Specialty of Genoa.
TORTELLI	Half-moon shaped pasta envelopes.
alla Lombarda:	Stuffed with pumpkin, macaroons, mustard, lemon & cheese.
alla Bolognese:	Stuffed with pork, veal, turkey, ham, cheese, brains, egg & nutmeg.
TORTIGLIONE	Almond cakes.
TORTINI DI RICOTTA	Ricotta cheese, parmesan cheese, flour, nutmeg & parsley. Rolled in egg &

ITALIAN

	crumbs & fried. A cheese croquette.
TOSCANA	Tuscany style.
Agnello con piselli alla:	Pot-roast leg of lamb with garlic & rosemary inserted in skin. Tomatoes & oil. Peas.
Finocchiona:	Salami with fennel.
Intingolo di maiale e uccelletti alla:	Stewed pork rind & tails with grilled spatchcock songbirds.
Arista di Maiale alla:	Roast pork with black-eyed beans.
Minestre Ceci:	Soup of chick peas, rosemary, garlic, anchovies, tomatoes & pasta.
Minestrone:	Soup of haricot beans, herbs, endive, tomatoes, cheese, onion, parsley, celery & pasta.
Trippa alla moda:	Tripe in oil with onion, garlic, marjoram, parsley, ham, wine, tomatoes, cheese & stock.
TOSTINI	Toast.
TOTANI	Squids.
TOURNEDOS	A steak cut from the eye of the fillet of beef. (About 4 ozs — 100 grams).
TRANCE	Slice.
TRACINA	Weaver fish.
TRASTEVERINA Bavette alla:	Pasta with anchovies, tuna & mushrooms.
TRENETTE	Pasta thickness of a match but long. A Genovese pasta served with pesto.

DINERS' DICTIONARY

TRIGLIE	Red mullet. Similar to Goatfish in U.S.A.
TRIPPA	Tripe. Beef stomach.
alla Bolognese:	In oil with onion, garlic, parley, meat sauce, cheese & lean pork. Butter.
alla Genovese:	In oil with ham, onions, garlic, wine, parsley, rosemary, tomatoes, cheese & stock.
alla Milanese:	In oil with onion, garlic, parsley, cheese & a lot of meat sauce.
moda Borghese:	In butter with onion, carrot, mushrooms, garlic, herbs & stock.
alla Romana:	In oil & butter with onion, garlic, parsley, cheese, chicken stock & chopped mint.
alla Toscana:	In oil with ham, onion, garlic, wine, parsley, marjoram, tomatoes, cheese & stock.
TROTA SALMONATA	Salmon trout.
TROTELLE	Trout.
all'Italiana:	Baked with fennel & wine.
TRUN	Literally "thunder". Fat yellow mushrooms of Piedmont.

U

UBBRIACATO	Literally "tipsy". Cooked with wine.
UCCELLETTI	Small birds of all kinds.
UCCELLI SCAPPATI	Literally "flying birds". Slices of sirloin rolled in ham & sage. On skewers with bread & salt pork. Grilled.
UMBRIA	Pasta sauce of oil, garlic, tomatoes,

ITALIAN

	truffles & anchovies.
UMIDO	Stewed.
UOVA	Eggs.
affrogate:	Poached.
barzotte:	Soft-boiled.
farcite:	Stuffed.
fritte:	Fried.
al guscio:	In their shells — boiled. (IN SORPRESSA means "surprise". Eggs are drained through small holes, mixed with meat sauce, cream & wine & put back in shells. Then boiled).
al piatto:	Baked in a fireproof dish.
rimestate:	Scrambled.
semidure:	Soft-boiled.
sode:	Hard-boiled.
strapassate:	Scrambled.
nelle tazzine:	Coddled.
UOVA DI TONNO	Dried & salted eggs of tuna fish. Sardinian specialty.
UVA	Grapes.
UVA PASSOLINA	Sultanas soaked in brandy & wrapped in lemon leaves.
UVETTA	Sultanas.

V

VACCINARA Coda di bue alla:	Oxtail stewed with vegetables, stock, herbs, wine, tomatoes, pine nuts & raisins.
VACHERIN	Rounds of meringue with cream, fresh fruit etc.

DINERS' DICTIONARY

VANIGLIA	Vanilla.
VECCHIO	Means old. For parmesan cheese — over 2 years old.
Vecchione:	Over 3 years old.
Stravecchione:	Over 4 years old.
VELLUTATE	French "velouté". Literally "velvet". A soup made with stock, flour, egg yolk & cream. Rather special.
VENERE	Cockles. Bi-valve mollusc.
VENETA	Specialty of the Veneto. The basin of the Po & Brenta rivers.
Minestre:	1: Soup of red haricot beans, ham, onions, cinnamon & noodles.
Minestre:	2: Soup of sausage, turnip, ham, cheese & rice.
Risotto:	Rice dish with fish stock, mussels & garlic.
VENEZIANA	Style of Venice.
Risotto in Capro Roman:	Rice dish with mutton, tomatoes, wine, cheese. (Venice in spite of name).
Risotto di secole:	Rice dish with beef & veal scraps, wine, celery & carrot.
Fegato di Vitello:	Thin strips of liver fried. Onions.
VENTRESCA	Belly or stomach. The choice cut of tuna fish.
VENTRICINA	Sausage of pork stomach, orange, fennel & peppers.
VERDE—I	Green.
Risotto:	Rice dish with spinach, celery, carrot, onion & meat sauce.
VERDURE TRITATE	Mixed herbs. French "Fines herbes".
VERMICELLI	Pasta similar but smaller than spaghetti. This is the size usually available under this name but other definitions have been given.
con le vongole:	With small clams.

ITALIAN

VERONESE Risotto:	Style of Verona. Simple rice dish with ham. Mushroom sauce.
VERZATA alla Milanese:	Cabbage soup. With savoy cabbage, sausage, onion, carrot, celery, parsley, sage, cheese. Toast.
VERZE RIPIENE	Cabbage leaves stuffed & cooked in oil or stock.
VILLA SASSI	Name of the home of Luigi Carnacina, a great Italian chef.
Ananasso:	Bananas hot, prepared at table with sliced pineapple, rum, Aurum liqueur, kirsch, hot chocolate sauce, almonds & ice cream.
Astaco:	Lobster grilled with vermouth, marsala, cream, onion & pepper sauce.
Asticciole di pollo:	Pieces of chicken, ham & sage on skewers. White wine, tomatoes & truffles. Served with tagliarini (pasta).
Spiedini di scampi:	Large shrimp tails on skewers grilled., With brandy, Worcester sauce, anchovy butter, mustard & lemon juice.
Filetti di Tacchino:	Roast & chopped breast of turkey, mixed with onion, sage, mushrooms, eggs. Rolled in ham & baked. On toast. Wine sauce.
VILLEROY Costolettine d'agnello alla:	Lamb chops with Villeroy & tomato sauces.
Salsa:	Egg yolk sauce with ham & truffle essence.

DINERS' DICTIONARY

VINO	Wine.
Abboccato:	Medium-sweet.
Bianco:	White.
Dolce:	Sweet.
Nero:	Red in Sicily or Sardinia.
Rosato:	Rosé.
Rosso:	Red.
Secco:	Dry.
VITE	Vine.
VITELLO	Veal. Young milk-fed calf.
Bracioline di:	Thin slices.
Costoletto-ini di:	Cutlets or chops.
Grenadine di:	Small steaks.
Involtini di:	Thin slices rolled & stuffed.
Medaglioni di:	Small steaks. French "medallions".
Messicani di:	Stuffed rolls.
Noce di:	Rolled rump.
Nodini di:	Chops.
Paillard di:	A steak very thin & grilled.
Petto di:	Breast.
Piccata di:	Small thin slices.
Saltimbocci di:	Thin slices folded in half, stuffed & fixed with a toothpick.
Scaloppine di:	Small thin slices. Same as PICCATA.
Spalla di:	Shoulder.
Teneroni di:	End of rib with breast meat. Riblets.
VITELLO TONNATO	Cold veal with tuna fish sauce.
VITELLONE	Young beef. Under three years old. From cattle that has never been worked.
VONGOLE	Small clams.

Z

ZABAIONEE	Zabaglione. A sweet made with egg yolks, sugar & sweet marsala wine whipped together. Served warm.
ZAFFERANO	Saffron. The stigma (& style) of autumn crocus. 1 million flowers = 1 lb saffron.
ZAMPA–E	Foot (of bird).
ZAMPONE	Stuffed pigs foot. (Modena).
ZENZERO	Ginger.
ZEPPOLE	Fried dough rings with sugar.
alla Napoletana:	Neopolitan puffs.
ZIMINO	A fish stew of Genoa. Oil, onion, parsley, celery, fennel, beet greens, cuttlefish, squid, fish, peppers & tomatoes.
ZITA	Pasta. Like large maccheroni.
ZITONE	As ZITA but larger still.
ZUCCA	Pumpkin.
ZUCCHERO	Sugar.
ZUCCHINI	Zucchini or courgettes. Small marrows.
ZUSO	Brawn with lemon juice.
ZUPPA-E	Soups mostly made of vegetables & with pasta or bread. The main exceptions are:
Inglese:	With tripe. BUT can be a sweet — Trifle.
alla Marinara:	Fish stew.
Pavese:	Clear soup with eggs poached in it. Cheese & fried bread.
di pesce:	Fish stew.
di Telline:	Mussel soup.

WINE DRINKING IN ITALY

The title is meant to draw attention to the fact that there is a considerable difference between drinking wine in Italy and drinking Italian wines elsewhere. The classification and legislation of their names for wines has been tightened up considerably in the last few years but there is still some degree of hit or miss when interpreting any label other than those of international reputation. Italy is probably the largest wine growing country in the world; though its output in some years may be less than that of France, it is usually greater and there is practically no part of the country in which the wine grape is not cultivated — often in a quite different manner from that by the French. Much wine is made by the same techniques as in France but there can be two major variations — from a single area the wine may be made by slightly different methods and the various products subsequently amalgamated so that the final product is in fact a blend rather than a single produce. Secondly a lot of wine such as Vino Santo or Passito is made from sun-dried grapes which is a technique used very rarely in France.

The Italians regard wine as something to be drunk and not talked or written about — they also consider it to be a necessary accompaniment to any meal. When eating out it often is most rewarding to ask for a carafe of wine and this is almost always available in a 'trattoria,' though not necessarily in a 'ristorante' if it considers itself too superior. It is interesting how many eating establishments outside mainland Europe now serve wine by the carafe and even the up-market hotels usually have a relatively cheap in-house wine. There are a few basic words needed for this exercise and the most important phrase is "Vino in Caraffa" which is pronounced exactly as written. It is necessary to specify which color and that too is quite simple:

ITALIAN

> Rosso means Red.
>
> Nero means dark Red. Used mostly in Sicily and Sardinia.
>
> Rosato means pink but Rosé (pronounced "Rosay") is sometimes used and always understood.
>
> Bianco means white. (pronounced "Beeankoh").

It is probably safer to take the carafe red wines than the white as on the whole the quality will be more acceptable to the taste of the average non-Italian.

There are a few more words which are useful both in asking for wine and in attempting to understand the importance of a label if purchasing:

> Secco (pronounced "Sekkoh") means dry.
>
> Abbocato means medium-sweet.
>
> Amabile (pronounced "Amabilay") means the same thing.
>
> Dolce (pronounced "Dolchay") means sweet and when an Italian says sweet, he really means it. Do not be confused by the well-known wine "Dolceaqua" which literally means "sweet water" and is a straightforward medium red wine or "Dolcetto" which is in fact a quite dry carafe wine of Piedmont.
>
> Amaro means bitter or very dry.

The phrases Vino da banco, Vino ordinario and Vino da tavola all mean ordinary wine which is often not bottled but served in the "caraffo" straight from the cask. This too is one of the variable features of Italian wines — they are kept for different lengths of time in a cask before bottling and when no control guidance is being offered this can account for quite large alterations of flavor between apparently identical bottles. Mostly the Italians seem to drink wine very young indeed and in fact the presence of any kind of deposit in a bottle might be thought by them to mean it is well past drinking. It is possible however that it may have been kept in the cask for a long time and that some other nationalities might feel that it has "gone over" in the cask instead of being allowed to mature in the bottle. The wine drinker has to learn that every country has its own tastes and that these do not always coincide either with his own pleasures or prejudices.

In a short survey of wines available it would be improper not to mention (and we almost said dismiss) the sparkling wines of Italy. The word Spumante (pronounced "spewmantay") means sparkling and the word Frizzante (pronounced "frizantay") means somewhat fizzy or as the French would say — "pétillant". The sparkling wines are seldom made by the champagne method though usually they are the result of a secondary ferment rather than some artifically inspired gassiness (regretably not always). The lack of persistance of the bubbles in the glass may give some indication of this and less than five seconds is possibly a good reason for feeding the nearest pot plant with such a delicacy. South-east of Turin is a sub-alpine area called Moscato d'Asti (south of the town of Asti) from which Moscato d'Asti Spumante is produced and is famous the world over as Asti Spumante. It is a relatively cheap sparkling white wine of fairly low alcohol content and rather sweet — it appeals to some people. There are a number of sparkling red wines made in Italy of which probably the best known is Lambrusco which comes from the Po valley near Modena. These are not wines that everyone would care to take with food and are possibly enjoyed by those who like them as a drink to be taken either before or after a meal.

There are a few more Italian words which are of significance. With tighter legislation there are now three official designations of wine:

> Denominazione Semplice — simple table wine.
> Denominazione di Origine Controllata — tested & conforming to a standard.
> Denominazione Constrollata e Garantita — the best wines.

These statements on the bottle will at least assist in deciding if the price bears some relationship to the likely quality of the contents.

To comment on the wines that may be encountered in Italy is to lay oneself open to being wrong almost all the time; it is

ITALIAN

difficult even to say if a given name will be a white wine or red let alone whether it be sweet or dry and to add to the confusion the wine may be named after the town where it is made or the grape from which it is derived. The simplest way to deal with this is to split the country into a few large areas — the specialty section mentions a few wines of each region but in this chapter we give it a rather wider sweep.

The north-west of Italy which contains the three great cities of Turin, Milan and Genoa is a prolific wine producing area of which a lot is converted into the vermouths for which the region is famous. It is also from this area that the most famous of the sparkling wines originate. The Nebbiola grape is responsible for Barola which is probably one of the best Italian red wines but also produces many others of less well-known names which may well refer to the grape on the bottle. The coastal strip produces the red wines Dolceaqua and Rossese and from Lombardy come Clastidio, Buttafuoco and Barbacarlo. The red wines must be judged by the Barola and its sister Barbaresco which is usually a little drier. These are named from the place whereas Freisa, Barbera and Grignolino are named from the grape.

White wines are made from the Vermentino grape amongst others and Cinqueterre, Polcevera and Coronata are well-known and drink well with the local fish dishes.

The north-eastern part of Italy is much influenced by Austria and Yugoslavia with a large amount of its production of wine being exported to the former. Two great names predominate — Soave as a white wine and Valpolicella as a red wine. They have in common that both do need drinking while quite young as with aging they lose some of their character. Inferno, Grumello and Sassella are produced from the Nebbiola grape but are different from the Barola of the north-west. Merlot and Refosco grapes produce a great deal of the red wine and are named on the bottles. The grape Schiava ia responsible for Santa Maddalena. Around Trento a number of red wines are named from the villages such as Teroldego, Marzemino, Negrara and Valagarina. Near Brescia the villages of Botticino, Franciacorta and Cellatica give a light red wine which is almost a rosé. The white wines come mostly from the Sylvaner, Sauvignon and the Reisling grape under many different names and varying from dry to very sweet. Gambellara is similar to Soave and Torcolata is a dessert wine from Vicenza.

The main names to remember in this region are Soave which is a light colored dryish white wine of considerable merit and drinkable with any part of a meal and the equally famous Valpolicella which is of a cherry color light flavored and has a dry almost bitter after-taste.

Central Italy which covers the peninsula from north of Florence to south of Rome and includes Sardinia is a prolific wine producing area and immediately below Florence is the famous Chianti producing area. In spite of the overwhelming fame of Chianti more white wines are produced than red and the Island of Elba is well known for Procanico and other white wines. The tiny island of Giglio produces Ansonica though the island does make some less than perfect wines. Vernaccia is a good dry white wine made on the mainland and also in Sardinia. From the north of the area is Montecarlo which can also be a red wine. The best known white wines are however Orvieto and Frascati — the former is a fairly sweet wine and some people might feel that it is almost the only sweet wine that is an acceptable accompaniment to fish and pasta — whilst Frascati which is made near Rome is strong, dry and fragrant. Verdicchio, Bianchello and Nuragus (from Sardinia) are other less well-known whites.

The red wine of the region is Chianti which comes from a strictly defined area in order to be classified as Chianti Classico and when so registered bears the black cockerel which is the symbol on the official label. It is aged in oak barrels and bottled in the special straw-covered flask or, now much more commonly, in the square shouldered Bordeaux bottles. Bought in caraffa around Florence it may well be slightly frizzante. Very considerable quantities of Chianti are produced but other notable red wines are Sangiovese, Montepulciano, Torgiano, Cannonau and the heavy over-sweet Sardinian wine Oliena.

ITALIAN

Southern Italy starts just above Naples and includes that marvellous island of Sicily. It would be impossible to discuss the wines of this section without commencing with Marsala. This is theoretically a white wine (it is of course dark grey or brown) made from sun-dried grapes (and as it is fortified by adding a stronger spirit, is perhaps not technically a wine) and is an incredibly good aperitif. It is made in Sicily where all the wines seem to us to be very strong and sweet but the effect of any drink depends to some extent on the climate and even more on the quality of the people — Sicily has to be at the top of the league on both counts. To us it is not a drink to accompany food but we may well be in a minority on this count. The islands of Ischia and Capri both produce white wines and the former a certain amount of red also. From the slopes of the volcano Vesuvius comes the famous Lacrima Christi which is usually a white wine but may also be red — it seems very variable. Falerno is a dry white and Aleatico a sweet. Asprinio is a white wine that is not quite so strong as some of the local products.

Ravello produce red and white wine as does Ciro. Aglianico is a dark red wine and Bari is famous for its Rosé. The island of Lipari produces both red and white. Many wines are produced in small areas which are very local.

This section opened by indicating the difference between drinking in Italy and buying Italian wines elsewhere and we have probably indicated the degree of confusion which can afflict the visitor particularly if he has become accustomed to the very strict regulations which apply in France. Such regulation does apply largely to the Italian wines purchased in London or New York but a journey through Tuscany can be a constant wine surprise. The drinking should be done as a minor adventure and not as a serious piece of gastronomic research; though the traditions and craft of the wine maker in Italy are as important as elsewhere they are much more obscure to the casual visitor and it is impossible for an outsider to do much to lead a way through the labyrinth but like any other maze it is great fun having a go. The one certain thing is that much of the wine is very good and is best when drunk in its own country.

TOWN INDEX TO SPECIALTY SECTIONS

Agrigento	SICILY	Brindisi	APULIA
Albano	LATIUM	Brisighella	EMILIA
Albenga	LIGURIA		
Alessandria	APULIA	Cagliari	SARDINIA
Alghero	SARDINIA	Campobasso	ABRUZZI
Amalfi	CAMPANIA	Canosa di	
Anagni	LATIUM	Puglia	APULIA
Ancona	MARCHES	Capri	CAMPANIA
Anzio	LATIUM	Capua	CAMPANIA
Aosta	PIEDMONT	Carrara	TUSCANY
Aquila	ABRUZZI	Caserta	CAMPANIA
Arezzo	TUSCANY	Cassino	LATIUM
Ascoli Piceno	MARCHES	Catania	SICILY
Assisi	UMBRIA	Catanzaro	CALABRIA
Atri	ABRUZZI	Cava de	
		Tirreni	CAMPANIA
Bari	APULIA	Cefalu	SICILY
Barletta	APULIA	Cesena	EMILIA
Bassano del		Chieti	ABRUZZI
Grappa	VENETIA	Cingoli	MARCHES
Bellagio	LOMBARDY	Citta di	
Belluno	VENETIA	Castello	TUSCANY
Benevento	CAMPANIA	Cividale del	
Bergamo	LOMBARDY	Fruili	VENETIA
Biella	PIEDMONT		GUILIA
Bitonto	APULIA	Civitavecchia	LATIUM
Bologna	EMILIA	Como	LOMBARDY
Bolzano	VENETIA	Conegliano	VENETIA
	TRIDENTINA	Cortona	TUSCANY
Brescia	LOMBARDY	Cosenza	CALABRIA
Bressanone	VENETIA	Cremona	LOMBARDY
	TRIDENTINA	Crotone	CALABRIA

ITALIAN

Elba	TUSCANY	Lucera	APULIA
Enna	SICILY		
		Mantua	
Fabriano	MARCHES	(Mantova)	LOMBARDY
Faenza	EMILIA	Marsala	SICILY
Fano	MARCHES	Matera	LUCANIA
Feltre	VENETIA	Merano	VENETIA
Fermo	MARCHES		TRIDENTINA
Ferrara	EMILIA	Messina	SICILY
Fidenza	EMILIA	Milan	
Florence		(Milano)	LOMBARDY
(Firenze)	TUSCANY	Milazzo	SICILY
Foggia	APULIA	Modena	EMILIA
Foligno	UMBRIA	Monreale	SICILY
Fondi	LATIUM	Montagnana	VENETIA
Forli	EMILIA	Montecatini	
Frascati	LATIUM	Terme	TUSCANY
		Monte	
Gaeta	LATIUM	pulciano	TUSCANY
Gela	SICILY	Monte Sant	
Genoa		Angelo	APULIA
(Genova)	LIGURIA	Monza	LOMBARDY
Gorizia	VENETIA		
	GIULIA	Naples	
Gubbio	UMBRIA	(Napoli)	CAMPANIA
		Narni	UMBRIA
Herculaneum		Noto	SICILY
(Ercolano)	CAMPANIA	Novara	PIEDMONT
		Nuoro	SARDINIA
Ischia	CAMPANIA		
Ivrea	PIEDMONT	Olbia	SARDINIA
		Orvieto	UMBRIA
Lecce	APULIA		
Leghorn		Padua	
(Livorno)	TUSCANY	(Padova)	VENETIA
Lerici	LIGURIA	Palermo	SICILY
Lipari	SICILY	Parma	EMILIA
Lucca	TUSCANY	Pavia	LOMBARDY

DINERS' DICTIONARY

Penna	ABRUZZI	Spezia	LIGURIA
Perugia	UMBRIA	Spoleto	UMBRIA
Pesaro	MARCHES	Sulmona	ABRUZZI
Piacenza	EMILIA	Syracuse	
Piazza		(Siracusa)	SICILY
Armerina	SICILY		
Pisa	TUSCANY	Taormina	SICILY
Pistoia	TUSCANY	Taranto	CALABRIA
Pompeii	CAMPANIA	Tempio	
Portofino	LIGURIA	Pausania	SARDINIA
Potenza	LUCANIA	Teramo	ABRUZZI
Prato	TUSCANY	Terni	LATIUM
Procida	CAMPANIA	Terracina	LATIUM
		Tivoli	LATIUM
Rapallo	LIGURIA	Todi	UMBRIA
Ragusa	SICILY	Trani	APULIA
Ravenna	EMILIA	Trapani	SICILY
Reggio di		Trent	
Calabria	CALABRIA	(Trento)	VENETIA
Reggio nell			TRIDENTINA
Emilia	EMILIA	Treviso	VENETIA
Rieti	LATIUM	Trieste	VENETIA
Rimini	EMILIA		GIULIA
Rome (Roma)	LATIUM	Turin	
Rovigo	VENETIA	(Torino)	PIEDMONT
San Marino	Republic	Udine	VENETIA
San Miniato	TUSCANY		GIULIA
San Remo	LIGURIA	Urbino	MARCHES
Santa Mari			
Capua Vetere	CAMPANIA	Varese	LOMBARDY
Saronno	LOMBARDY	Venice	
Sarzana	LIGURIA	(Venezia)	VENETIA
Sassari	SARDINIA	Ventimiglia	LIGURIA
Savona	LIGURIA	Vercelli	PIEDMONT
Sciacca	SICILY	Verona	VENETIA
Siena	TUSCANY	Viareggio	TUSCANY
Sorrento	CAMPANIA	Vicenza	VENETIA

ITALIAN

Viterbo   LATIUM   Volterra   TUSCANY
Vittorio
Veneto   VENETIA

REGIONS OF ITALY AND SPECIALTY DISHES

ABRUZZI AND MOLISE

In South-central Italy bordering the Adriatic and in the high mountainous part of the Apennines. Narrow gorges, high chalky mountains and wild forests with a harsh climate. There are no large cities and Aquila, Campobasso and Chieti are the largest towns.

Vines, almonds and olives are grown in the sheltered areas and in drained marshes maize and tomatoes are cultivated in quantity.

The main specialties of the region are:

Pasta
Maccheroni alla Chitarra.	Hand made pasta strips with lamb sauce.
Pincingrassi.	Pasta oven cooked with meat gravy & cream added.

Fish
Scapece.	Fish pickled with saffron.

Meat
Cosciotto d'agnello all'Abruzzese.	Leg of lamb braised with rosemary, garlic, white wine & tomatoes.
Mazzarella.	Lamb offal, egg & spices.

Cheese
Littecini.	Fresh mountain cheese.

Wine
"d'Abruzzo".	Several red & white local wines.
Trebbiano d'Abruzzo.	Dry white wine.

APULIA

The south-eastern part of the peninsula which forms the "heel of the boot". The principal towns are Bari, Brindisi, Foggia, Lecce and Trani.

Moderate cultivation in the plain around Bari. Wheat, vines and olives are grown, and salt and chemicals are mined. Some grazing is available and sheep, horses, cattle and pigs form important produce. Almonds, lemons, oranges and tobacco are grown.

The main specialties of the region are:

Cerignola.	Large green olives.
Capretto ripieno al forno.	Roast kid stuffed with herbs.

CALABRIA

The "toe" of Italy. Mountains covered with forests. Good pastures. Earthquakes have occurred in the past. Catanzaro, Reggio, Taranto and Cosenza are the main towns.

A fertile coastal strip on which vines, olives & fruit are grown.

The main specialties of the region are:

Almost any unknown name will prove to be a local pasta of unusual shape e.g. Stivaletti — "little boots"!

Ostriche.	Oysters of Taranto a local specialty.
Capretto ripieno al forno.	Roast kid stuffed with herbs.
Bergamot.	A citrus fruit. Citrus bergamia.
Solazzi.	Liquorice.
Corigliano.	Liquorice juice.

ITALIAN

Wine
There are some local red and white wines.

CAMPANIA

The south-western part of the peninsula. Bordered on the north by Lazio and Abruzzi, north-east by Apulia, east by Lucania and west by the Mediterranean. Naples, Caserta and Salerno are the main towns. There is a large fertile plain between the mountains and the sea. Many mineral springs in the area.

Cotton spinning and weaving are important. Shipbuilding is a major industry. Food factories, particularly for pastas.

The main specialties of the region are:

Pasta and Savories

Calzone imbottito.	Half-moon containers of pizza dough filled with ham & cheese & baked.
Lasagne alla Napolitana:	Pasta with cheese & ham braised in marsala.
Linguine aglio e olio.	Pasta with oil & garlic.
Maccheroni ai quattro formaggi.	Pasta with four cheese.
Mozzarella in Carrossa.	Cheese savory.
Panzarotti.	Dough with ham & cheese fried in oil.
Pizza.	Pizza dough with cheese, tomatoes, anchovies, marjoram & capers.

Meat

Costata OR Bistecche alla Pizzaiola.	Fillet steak with tomatoes, garlic & marjoram.
Sartu.	Rice pie with meat & herbs.

ALSO — All dishes
 "alla NAPOLITANA".
 "alla CAPRESE".

Wine

Capri (from the Island).	Red and white.
Ischia (from the Island).	White.
From Vesuvius.	Lacrima Christi — white.
	Gragano — red.

EMILIA

The north-central part of Italy bordering the northern Adriatic. Venetia and Lombardy to the north, Liguria to the west, Tuscany to the south and the Marches to the south-east with the Adriatic sea to the east. There are large plains in the northern parts of the region. Bologna, Modena and Parma are among the principal towns.

An extremely fertile region with many important products — cereals, vegetables, wine, rice and beet. Flax and silk. Mulberries. Eels.

The main specialties of the region are:

Pasta etc.

Passatelli.	Similar to pasta — made from breadcrumbs. Cut like spaghetti. Served in soups.
Pasta alla Bolognese:	With meat, gravy & tomato sauce (RAGU).

Meat and Birds

Bomba di riso.	Oven cooked pigeons with rice.
Bondiola.	Cured shoulder of pork with wine.
Capocolla.	Cured shoulder of pork.
Culatello.	Parma ham.
Modena Zampone.	Pig trotters or feet.
Mortadelle.	Pork sausage. May be mixture of pork, veal, tripe & potatoes.

Prosciutto di Parma.	Lightly salted — not smoked — ham.
Salami.	Sausage.
ALSO — see "alla BOLOGNESE". "alla MODENESE".	

Cheese

Parmigiano.	Parmesan.
Grana.	Generic name for parmesan type of cheese.

Wine

Lambrusco.	Sparkling red wine.
Albano.	White wine.

LATIUM (LAZIO)

That region in the western southern part of the peninsula of which Rome is the center. Famous for the pastures resulting in high sheep production and horses.

The main specialties of the region are:

Pasta etc.

Fettucine.	Strip maccheroni.
Gnocchi.	Different from gnocchi di semolina in that it is made from potatoes.

Meat

Abbachio al forno.	Roast baby lamb.
Saltimbocca.	Veal fillet in ham, fried in butter. With marsala & sage.

Vegetables

Carciofi alla guida.	Artichokes in oil with garlic & parsley.
Fave al Guaciale.	Broad or shell beans with onions & bacon.

DINERS' DICTIONARY

ALSO — see "alla ROMANA".
Cheese
Fionne Molli.   Soft, bright yellow.
Pecorino.   Sheep's cheese.
Wine
Est!Est!Est!   White wine of Montefioscone.
Castelli Romani.   White and red wines.
Frascati   Probably the best of the white wines.

LIGURIA

Extends as a thick coastal strip from the French border, round the gulf of Genoa as far as Spezia. The Alps are to the north and the sea to the south. Genoa, Spezia and Savona are the main towns.

A fertile and floriferous area. Maize, wine, oranges, lemons, other fruit, olives, potatoes, peaches & flowers. Important for mining of copper, manganese and iron. Engineering, manufacturing and shipbuilding.

The main specialties of the region are:

Pesto.   Characteristic of genoese cooking. A blend of oil, herbs, onions, nuts, garlic, spinach & cheese.

Soup
Pistou.   Fried beans, potatoes & tomatoes. With vermicelli, garlic, basil & tomatoes.

Zuppa di datteri.   Shellfish soup.
Savories
Crostate salte alla Genovese.   Tart of beet greens, cheese & marjoram.

Focaccia.	Type of bread or pizza made with oil & salt to be eaten with cheese.
Sardenara.	Type of pizza.

Fish

Bagioi.	Snails in mint & tomato sauce.
Burrida.	Fish stew.
Cappon Magro.	A very variable fish salad. A filling garlic dish. See main entry.
Calamaretti in Zimino.	Squid with chopped beet greens.
Zimino	Fish stew of Genoa.

Meat

Cima.	Cold veal stuffed with pork, cheese, turnips, peas, sweetbreads, brains, nuts, eggs, artichokes & marjoram.

ALSO — see "alla GENOVESE".

Wine

Cinqueterre and Coronata.	Strong white wines.
Scicchetra.	Similar to the above.
Dolceacqua.	Strong dark red wine.

LOMBARDY

The north-central part of mainland Italy with the Alps and Switzerland to the north, Piedmont to the west, Venetia to the east and Emilia to the south. The principal towns are Milan, Bergamo, Brescia, Como and Pavia. Most of the Italian lakes are in Lombardy.

Vines, fruit and nut trees, mulberries and silkworms. Grain and flax on the plains. Milan is a famous silk market and Como is famous for silk weaving. Engineering and manufacturing.

DINERS' DICTIONARY

The main specialties of the region are:

Meat

Bresaola.	Dried salt beef. Antipasta with oil, lemon juice & parsley.
Casoeula or Cazzuola.	Stewed pork sausage, bacon & cabbage.

Miscellaneous

Mostarda di frutta.	Fruit in syrup with garlic & mustard.
Panettone.	Fruit cake.
Polenta pasticciata.	Polenta, white sauce & mushrooms oven baked with cheese.

ALSO — see "alla MILANESE". Many dishes amongst which — minestrone, risotto, costoletta and osso buco are very well known.

   "alla PAVESE".
   "alla LOMBARDI".

Cheese

Bel Paese.	Soft & mild.
Bitto.	Cow & goat milk cheese.
Crescenza.	Cow cheese. Creamy yellow. Only in winter.
Gorgonzola.	Blue herbed cow cheese.
Lodi Grana.	Lombardy equivalent of Parmesan.
Robiola.	Soft & runny with red casing. Fresh or old.

Wine

Sassella, Grumelli & Inferno.	Red Bordeaux type.
Frecciarossa.	Red & white wines of quality.

ITALIAN

LUCANIA (BASILICATA)

The central-southern part of the peninsula of Italy. There are no large towns and Potenza is the principal one.

Very mountainous region producing wheat, olives and chestnuts. Ginger is used a great deal in the cooking.

The main specialties of the region are:

Chicken
Pollo alla Lucana:	Stuffed with livers, eggs & cheese.
Pollo alla Potentina.	Pieces cooked in oil, onions, red peppers, white wine, tomato & basil.

Wine
Aleatico di Puglia.	Sweet red wine from dried grapes.
Aglianico del Vulture.	Red table wine.
Asprino.	Dry white wine.

MARCHES

The eastern middle part of the peninsula. Emilia to the north, Abruzzi to the south, Umbria and Tuscany to the west and the Adriatic to the east. Principally hills and the limestone mountains of the Apennines. Ancona and Pesaro are the main towns.

Silk, grain, wine, olives and sugar refining. Brickworks and iron making. Sulfur mines.

The main wines of the region are:

Verdicchio.	A dry white wine named after the grape.
Moscato and San Giovese.	Wines of San Marino.

PIEDMONT

The north-western part of mainland Italy bordered to the north by the semi-circle of the Alps of Switzerland and France and to the east by the Lombardy plain. Turin, Cuneo, Alessandria and Aosta are among the principal towns.

Silk, cotton, wool and clothing manufacturing are important. Agriculture is a major industry with wheat, rice, maize, market gardening and wine production most fruitful. The proximity of mountains makes hydro-electrics a major occupation.

The main specialties of the region are:

Cooking is basically the same as the French with butter playing a major role.

Savories

Bagna Cauda.	A hot dip of garlic, anchovies & truffles for cardoons or celery. Traditional Christmas Eve.
Elaborati di formaggi.	Complex cheese mixtures on biscuits, bread or crackers.
Fonduta.	Melted cheese with milk, eggs & truffles.

Meat

Bollito misto.	Mixture of beef, lamb, veal & pork boiled with vegetables.

Vegetables

Cardi.	Cardoons with a hot sauce.
ALSO — see "alla PIEMONTESE".	

Cheese

Castelmagno.	Strong, salty & herbed.
Fontina.	Like a rich creamy gruyère.
Robiola.	Soft & runny with red casing. Fresh or old.

ITALIAN

Wine
Vermouth which is a fortified wine with herbs is made in quantity.

Barola and Barbaresco.	Red Burgundy type.
Barbera.	Strong dark red wine.
Nebbiolo.	Red wine named after the grape.
Freisa.	Red wine of Bordeaux type.
Grignolino.	Light sweet red wine.
Asti Spumante.	Sweet sparkling white wine. From Muscat grape.

SARDINIA

A large mountainous island west of the Italian peninsula and south of Corsica. Cagliari and Sassari are the main towns.

Mainly agricultural with a lot of livestock. Fishing is important with tuna fish and sardines being caught in quantity. Coal, iron, lead, salt and zinc are mined. Cotton growing is of increasing importance and cork is also produced.

The main specialties of the island are:

Soup
Succutunu. — A concentrated soup with semolina.

Fish
Filotrottas. — Eels cooked over charcoal on skewers.

Meat and Birds
Grive and Taccula. — Small birds. Cold or hot.
Porchetta. — Spit roasted suckling pig.
Prosciutto di Cinghiale. — Smoked wild boar ham.

Cheese etc.
Fetta. — Salty white crumbly cheese as in Greece.

DINERS' DICTIONARY

Formaggio Fiore.	A hard solid pecorino (sheep cheese).
Gioddu.	Yogurt.

Wine

Wines are strong in alcohol similar to Marsala.

Vernaccia.	Strong dry white wine.
Nuragus.	A lighter dry white wine.
Cannonau and Oliena.	Heavy sweet red wines.

SICILY

The largest island in the Mediterranean situated off the "toe" of Italy. Well populated with a number of large towns amongst which are Palermo, Messina, Agrigento and Syracuse.

Grain, fruit and nuts. Few livestock. Wine in quantity. Palermo is a large industrial and manufacturing city. Sulfur is mined and salt extracted. Swordfish, tuna fish and anchovies in abundance.

The main specialties of the island are:

Zuso.	Brawn with lemon juice.
Orecchiette ai broccoli.	Pasta with flowering broccoli.
Caponata.	Vegetable or cold antipasta. Fried aubergines or egg plant with capers, olives, celery, anchovies, onion, tomatoes, vinegar & parsley. With tuna, lobster or tuna roes.
Annelliti.	Rings of cuttlefish oven cooked.
Cuscusu.	Couscous. Specially prepared pelleted semolina with casseroled meat or

ITALIAN

	chicken and a hot spicy sauce. Possibly with fish.
Cassata.	Partly iced cream cake. Chocolate & candied fruit.

ALSO — see
  "alla SICILIANA"
  "alla PALERMITANA".

Cheese

Canestreto.	Sheeps cheese.

Wine

Marsala is the most famous product. Dark aperitif wine which is fortified and bears some resemblance to sherry.

Corvo.	Red and white.
Faro.	Red.
Val di Lupo.	White.
Lipari and Pantellaria (both islands).	Mostly white wines.
Mount Etna.	Mostly white wines.

TUSCANY

The western part of the center of the Italian peninsula with Liguria and Emilia to the north, Marches and Umbria to the east, Lazio to the south and the Mediterranean forming the western boundary. Florence (Firenze), Arezzo, Leghorn (Livorno), Pisa, Grosseto and Siena are amongst the main towns. Very fertile valley of the Arno.

Wheat, market garden produce, wine, olives, pumpkins and Lucca beans (from Lucca). Iron, copper and mercury, marble and ceramics.

The main specialties of the region are:

Fish

Baccala.	Dried cod with oil, garlic & pepper.
Cacciucco.	Fish soup or stew.
Triglie.	Red mullet or goatfish.

DINERS' DICTIONARY

Meat
Costata. — Veal grilled in oil.

Vegetables
Fagioli. — Beans served in oil, onions & herbs.

Sweet
Panforte. — Siena sugar cake with nuts, honey & fruit.

ALSO — see
  "alla FIORENTINA"
  "alla TOSCANA"
  "alla LIVORNESE".

Wine
Chianti is the most famous. — Red and white but principally red.

Santo Toscano. — Very sweet white wine.

UMBRIA

In the middle of the Italian peninsula with Tuscany and the Marches to the north and east with Lazio and Abruzzi to the south and west. The only region in the peninsula with no sea coast. Perugia and Terni are the main towns. Mountains, pastures and fertile valleys.

Olives and wine. Steelworks and chemicals. Wool, jute & cotton.

The main specialties of the region are:

Crostini di fegatini. — Stale bread trimmed & fried with chicken livers.

Porchetta. — Suckling pig roasted on a spit.

ALSO — see
  "alla PERUGINA".

Wine
Orvieto. — Dry or medium sweet white wine.

VENETIA

The large north-eastern part of mainland Italy which extends down to the Adriatic. It is divided into three parts:
1. Veneto or Venetia proper. This is the western section which borders Lake Garda. Contains the Po valley, Verona and Venice.
2. Venetia Guilia. The eastern portion. Udine is the capital and it borders with Trieste.
3. Venetia Tridentina or Trentino. This is the north-central part and has much German influence.

Cereals, vines, fruit and large pasture areas. Silk, rice and beet.

The main specialties of the region are:

Soup
Paparot.	Spinach soup with polenta (maize flour).

Rice etc.
Risi e bisi.	Rice and green peas.
Risotto in Capro Roman.	Rice dish with mutton, tomatoes, wine & cheese.
Polenta.	A boiled product made from maize flour used as a bread substitute.

Fish
Baccala Mantecato.	Creamy dried cod mixed with oil. Similar to French "brandade".
Molecche.	Fried small soft-shelled crabs. Eels and shellfish in various forms.

Meat
Fegato alla Veneziana.	Calves liver fried with onions.
Lepre alla Montanura.	Hare stewed in pine nuts & sultanas.

DINERS' DICTIONARY

ALSO — see "VENETA" "VENEZIANA."

Wine

Valpolicella.	A strong red wine of varying quality. Some very good indeed.
Caldaro & Marzemino.	Red.
Termino.	White.
Santa Maddalena.	Good red wine.
Bardolino & Valpenta.	Similar to Valpolicella.
Soave.	Widely known white wine.

ITALIAN

REGIONS OF ITALY.

1. Abruzzi
2. Apulia
3. Calabria
4. Campania
5. Emilia
6. Latium
7. Liguria
8. Lombardy
9. Lucania
10. Marches
11. Piedmont
12. Sardinia
13. Sicily
14. Tuscany
15. Umbria
16. Venetia